WELLINGTON

MILITARY PROFILES SERIES EDITOR

Dennis E. Showalter, Ph.D.
Colorado College

Instructive summaries for general and expert readers alike, volumes in the Military Profiles series are essential treatments of significant and popular military figures drawn from world history, ancient times through the present.

MILITARY PROFILES AVAILABLE

FORTHCOMING MILITARY PROFILES

WELLINGTON

The Iron Duke

Philip Haythornthwaite

Potomac Books, Inc.
Washington, D.C.

Library of Congress Cataloging-in-Publication Data
Haythornthwaite, Philip J.
  Wellington : the Iron Duke / Philip Haythornthwaite.
    p. cm. — (Military profiles series)
  Includes bibliographical references and index.
  ISBN-13: 978-1-57488-892-8 (alk. paper)
  ISBN-13: 978-1-57488-893-5 (pbk. : alk. paper)
  1. Wellington, Arthur Wellesley, Duke of, 1769–1852. 2. Great Britain—Politics and government—19th century. 3. Great Britain—History, Military—19th century. 4. Prime ministers—Great Britain—Biography. 5. Generals—Great Britain—Biography. I. Title.
  DA68.12.W4H39 2007
  941.081092—dc22
  [B]
                                    2006024099

Printed in the United States of America on acid-free paper that meets the American National Standards Institute Z39-48 Standard.

Potomac Books, Inc.
22841 Quicksilver Drive
Dulles, Virginia 20166

First Edition

10 9 8 7 6 5 4 3 2 1

Contents

Maps

On the morning of June 18, 1815, the Emperor Napoleon considered the enemy army that lay a short distance to the north of his own forces. With the confidence that had sustained him for some two decades of conflict, he declared to his companions that his opponent was a bad general in command of bad troops, and that the day's battle would be a picnic. He was wrong, and by that evening his regime was destroyed.

The general he underestimated, Arthur Wellesley, first Duke of Wellington, was in fact one of the greatest of all military commanders, and was arguably his nation's most outstanding personality during his lifetime. He was almost a precise contemporary of Napoleon's— Wellington was little more than a hundred days older—and his career in some respects had resembled that of the French emperor: both had achieved great prominence from relatively unpromising beginnings almost entirely by their own ability and industry. Napoleon had risen higher, creating an empire and giving his name to the period of his reign; but his fall was heavier because of it. Wellington's success had been achieved in the course of public service, which had also led to great personal advancement. As a general and military administrator, he was an acknowledged master of his craft, and was responsible to a very large degree for the creation of an army that he described as "probably the most complete machine for its numbers now existing in Europe," and he combined his military duties with the responsibilities of diplomacy.

Although his most notable successes were in the field of arms, culminating with a crucial role in the final defeat of Napoleon, in succeeding years he held his nation's highest civil as well as military office, and, ultimately, despite his proverbially reserved exterior, won a place in the hearts of his countrymen. Although his time at the head of his country's government did not mirror his military achievements, he transcended all difficulties to become an icon for his age, a personification of the concept of public duty, and one of his nation's greatest citizens. A measure of his position in society was the fact that in later life he was known commonly as simply "the Duke," as if no other dukes had ever existed. In terms of the peerage, there were other dukes, but in other respects, Wellington was quite unique.

Chronology

	May 4	Capture of Seringapatam
	May 6	Wellesley appointed governor of Seringapatam
	July 9	Wellesley appointed to govern Mysore
1800	September 10	Defeat of Doondiah Waugh at Conaghull
1801	July 17	Appointed Brigadier-General for expedition to Egypt (upon which he did not embark)
1802	April 29	Wellesley promoted to Major-General
1803	August 11	Capture of Ahmednuggur
	September 23	Wellesley's first major victory at Assaye
	November 29	Victory of Argaum
	December 15	Capture of Gawilghur
1804	September 1	Wellesley appointed Knight Companion of the Order of the Bath
1805	September 10	Wellesley returned to Britain
1806	January 30	Wellesley appointed Colonel of Thirty-third Regiment
	April 1	Elected as Member of Parliament (originally for Rye)
	April 10	Wellesley married the Honorable Catherine Pakenham
1807	February 3	Birth of eldest son, Arthur Richard Wellesley
	April 3	Wellesley appointed Secretary for Ireland
	April 8	Appointed to Privy Council
	August 29	Victory at Kjöge in expedition to Denmark
1808	January 16	Birth of second son, Charles
	April 25	Promoted to Lieutenant-General
	August 1	Landing at Mondego Bay, Wellesley in temporary command of British expedition to Portugal
	August 17	First victory in the Peninsula: over Delaborde at Roliça
	August 21	Victory over Junot at Vimeiro; then superseded in command by Sir Harry Burrard, and subsequently by Sir Hew Dalrymple
	August 30	Convention of Cintra

	November 22	Wellesley gave evidence before the Cintra inquiry following his return to Britain
1809	January 27	Vote of thanks in Parliament for Vimeiro, acknowledged by Wellesley in person
	March 7	Wellesley submitted his Memorandum for the Defense of Portugal
	April 6	Wellesley received notification of his command of the expedition to Portugal
	April 22	Wellesley assumed command in Portugal
	May 12	Passage of the Douro and capture of Oporto, maneuvering Soult out of Portugal
	July 6	Wellesley appointed Marshal-General of Portugal
	July 27–28	Victory of Talavera over Marshal Victor
	August 26	First step in the peerage: created Baron Douro of Wellesley and Viscount Wellington of Talavera and Wellington
	September 16	Wellesley used his new signature "Wellington" for the first time
	October 20	Wellington wrote his memorandum to Col. Richard Fletcher regarding the construction of the Lines of Torres Vedras to protect Lisbon
1810	September 27	Victory of Busaco against Massena
	October 14	A skirmish convinced Massena of the futility of attempting to pierce the Lines of Torres Vedras
1811	March 4	After starving in front of the Lines of Torres Vedras, Massena commenced his withdrawal from Santarem
	April 3	Action against the retreating French at Sabugal
	May 3–5	Victory at Fuentes de Oñoro against Massena
	May 16	Battle of Albuera
	July 31	Wellington appointed General (local rank)
	October 26	Wellington granted permission to accept the Portuguese peerage, Conde do Vimeiro

1812	January 19	Capture of Ciudad Rodrigo
	February 18	Wellington advanced in the peerage to Earl of Wellington; Spanish peerage as Duque de Ciudad Rodrigo
	April 6	Capture of Badajoz
	July 22	Victory of Salamanca over Marmont
	August 18	Wellington advanced in the peerage to Marquess of Wellington
	October 21	Wellington given permission to accept the appointment of generalissimo of Spanish army, offered to him on September 22
	October 21–22	Siege of Burgos abandoned
	December 7	Parliament awarded Wellington £100,000 to purchase an estate
	December 18	Wellington received Portuguese dukedom: Duque da Victoria
1813	January 1	Wellington became Colonel of the Royal Horse Guards
	March 4	Wellington awarded knighthood of the Order of the Garter
	June 21	Victory of Vitoria; Wellington's promotion to Field-Marshal backdated to this date
	July 25–31	Battles of the Pyrenees against Soult, the most significant being Sorauren, July 28
	September 8	Capture of San Sebastian
	October 7	Passage of the Bidassoa
	November 10	Victory of the Nivelle over Soult
	December 9	Victory of the Nive over Soult
1814	February 27	Victory of Orthez over Soult
	April 10	Victory of Toulouse over Soult
	May 3	Advanced in the peerage to Duke of Wellington
	July 5	Wellington appointed ambassador to France
1815	February 3	Wellington arrived in Vienna as British plenipotentiary to the Congress at that city
	April 5	Wellington took command of the forces in

	September 26	Death of Richard, Marquess Wellesley
1846	June 26	Corn Laws repealed by House of Lords
1852	September 14	Death of Duke of Wellington at Walmer Castle
	November 18	State funeral and burial at St. Paul's Cathedral

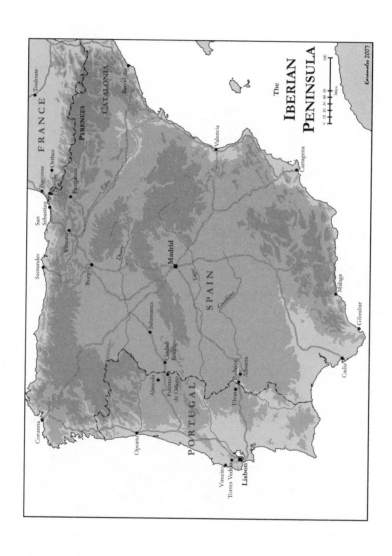

The

IBERIAN
PENINSULA

0 10 20 30 40 50   100
└─┴─┴─┴─┴─┴──────────────┘
          Miles

Kernamdes 2007

FRANCE

Toulouse

Bayonne
Orthez

San
Sebastian
Pamplona

PYRENEES

CATALONIA

Barcelona

Vittoria

Corunna

Santander

Burgos

Ebro

Duero

SPAIN

Valencia

Cartagena

Salamanca

Tagus

Madrid

Ciudad
Rodrigo

Almeida
Fuentes
de Oñoro

Guadiana

PORTUGAL

Elvas
Badajoz
Albuera

Málaga

Gibraltar

Oporto

Cadiz

Vimeiro
Torres Vedras
Lisbon

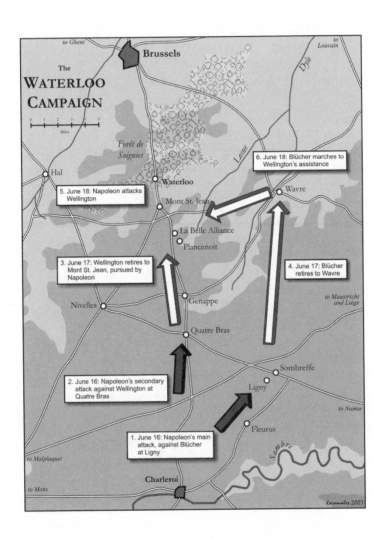

The Waterloo Campaign

Brussels

to Ghent

to Louvain

WATERLOO CAMPAIGN

The

0 1 2 3 4 5
Miles

Forêt de Soignies

Dyle

Lasne

Hal

Waterloo

Mont St. Jean

6. June 18: Blücher marches to Wellington's assistance

La Belle Alliance

Plancenoit

5. June 18: Napoleon attacks Wellington

Wavre

3. June 17: Wellington retires to Mont St. Jean, pursued by Napoleon

4. June 17: Blücher retires to Wavre

Genappe

to Maastricht and Liége

Nivelles

Quatre Bras

2. June 16: Napoleon's secondary attack against Wellington at Quatre Bras

Sombreffe

Ligny

to Namur

Fleurus

1. June 16: Napoleon's main attack, against Blücher at Ligny

Sombre

to Malplaquet

to Mons

Charleroi

Karamales 2007

WELLINGTON

"How Not to Do It": A Military Apprenticeship

I AM THINKING of the French that I am going to fight. I have not seen them since the campaign in Flanders, when they were capital soldiers, and a dozen years of victory under Buonaparte [*sic*] must have made them better still. They have besides, it seems, a new system of strategy, which has outmanoeuvered and overwhelmed all the armies of Europe . . . they may overwhelm me, but I don't think they will outmanoeuver me. First, because I am not afraid of them, as everyone else seems to be; and secondly, because if what I hear of their system of manoeuvers be true, I think it a false one against steady troops. I suspect all the continental armies were more than half beaten before the battle was begun. I, at least, will not be frightened beforehand.[1]

Such self-confidence was remarkable for a military commander entrusted with an independent command against a European enemy for the first time in his career and about to confront the most successful army in the continent. Even more remarkable is the fact that it was not misplaced, for the abilities from which it was engendered were to mark out the subject as one of the greatest military commanders of the age.

The future Duke of Wellington was born the Honorable Arthur Wesley on or around May 1, 1769, probably in his family's house on Merrion Street in Dublin.[2] He was the third son (of five, and one daughter) of Garret Wesley, Lord Mornington, who some nine years before had been advanced in the Irish peerage to Viscount Wellesley of Dangan Castle (the family seat in County Meath) and first Earl of Mornington, and his wife Anne, daughter of the first Viscount Dungannon. The Wellesley family (this old spelling supplanted "Wesley" again after Arthur's birth) was associated initially with Wellesley in Somerset, though their residence in Ireland dated from the mid-thirteenth century. From this fact, Arthur Wesley has been referred to as Irish, but he almost certainly never regarded himself as such. His family belonged to the landowning, ruling elite, considerably divorced from the indigenous population despite generations of residence. They were of English descent and Protestant among a predominantly Roman Catholic Irish population, perpetuating a rule that over the centuries had been a cause of conflict and bloodshed. The division had widened after the "Glorious Revolution" of 1688, when considerable restrictions had been laid on adherents to the Catholic faith—even an inability to hold military or naval commissions, at least in theory—and the underlying tensions in society might have led the Anglo-Irish landowners to regard their position as somewhat insecure. Under these conditions it is perhaps not surprising that as a child Arthur should form intensely conservative opinions and a belief that only strong government could guard against uprising and civil disorder, yet his acceptance that the legislation that discriminated against Roman Catholics was unsustainable was to lead to the most lasting of his political achievements.

Despite his social position, the Earl of Mornington was not wealthy. As a professor of music at Trinity College, Dublin, he had some success as a composer, but when he died in 1781 at the age of almost forty-six, the family finances were in so parlous a state that the new Lord Mornington—the eldest son, Richard—had to leave Oxford without a degree. Arthur, whose only skill at this stage appeared to be the inherited musical talent of playing the violin, was sent to Eton in 1781 but was taken away in 1784 so that the family funds could be concentrated on his two younger brothers, who seemed better prospects academically. For such an apparently untalented, unacademic, and solitary boy as Arthur, his career choice was limited; his mother described him as "awkward" and confessed that there was nothing else for him but the army.

Preparations for a military career were set in motion. Arthur was sent to the Royal Academy of Equitation at Angers in France, where a number of British aristocrats were educated. He was there for less than a year but the school had a profound impact on him. Arthur perfected his French and seems to have set his mind on a career in the military, even though the army was looked down upon by much of polite society. On March 7, 1787, he was appointed an ensign (the lowest commissioned rank) in the Seventy-third (Highland) Regiment of Foot.

At that time, the officer corps of the British army was largely restricted to sons of military families, the younger sons of aristocracy and gentry, or those sufficiently affluent to be able to afford the expenses involved; only the most provident middle-ranking officers and few subalterns could live off the pay they received. Advancement, especially in peacetime, usually involved the system of "purchase" by which an individual would buy his commission or promotion. The practice had many failings and many critics; one experienced officer stated that

> commissions were thrown away on persons unworthy of bearing them, or incapable of performing the duties . . . Boys at school . . . were field officers in the British army . . . while the son of a low, but opulent mechanic, by means of a bribe, saw himself at the head of a troop of horse, which he had neither the courage nor abilities to lead.[3]

In the House of Commons in 1795 Gen. Banastre Tarleton, who had forged his military reputation in America, claimed that "gold and rank . . . were now the only passports to preferment," citing the case of the Earl of Granard, "who jumped into the rank of Lieutenant-Colonel, and in seventeen days experience found himself qualified for the command of the army."[4] Until the purchase system was reformed, it denied promotion to many worthy officers who lacked money or influence but conversely permitted others to attain higher rank more rapidly than if promotion had depended on seniority or length of service.

To a degree, this was to be the case with Arthur Wesley, though his first advancement arose from his family background. His elder brother Richard, already making his way in government by a combination of connections and his own ability, secured for young Arthur the appointment of aide-de-camp to the Viceroy of Ireland barely seven months after he had first entered the army. He served in this position for several years, rising in rank step by step (lieutenant in December 1787, captain in June 1791), changing regiments as he went. His duties with the Viceroy must have provided an early insight into civil administration, and Arthur gained further experience when he succeeded his brother William in the family seat of Trim in the Irish Parliament, but his military service must have been minimal. His original regiment was in India at the time, so any service he undertook must have been merely with the regimental depot, and once part of the Viceroy's household he cannot have performed any military duties. It is evident, though, that he began to make a serious study of his profession. His failure to gain the hand in marriage of the Honorable Catherine (Kitty) Pakenham, daughter of the second Baron Longford, on the grounds of his poor financial prospects acted as a further spur to his advancement in the army. With a loan from his brother Richard he purchased a majority in the Thirty-third (First West Riding) Regiment in April 1793, and at about this time he made a profound break with his past by destroying his violin. Kitty Pakenham believed this was evidence of "great self-command and firmness of decision,"[5] and certainly it marked a change in his life: the somewhat gauche, dilettante young aristocrat was replaced by an officer determined to pursue his trade to the exclusion of frivolous pursuits.

In September 1793 Wesley purchased a further step in rank, to become lieutenant-colonel (and commanding officer) of the Thirty-third, the regiment with which he has become most associated and that, from 1853, bore his name as the Duke of Wellington's Regiment.

A regimental command presented a number of new challenges, including the task of straightening the regiment's chaotic accounts, at which, as later, he proved to be financially very adept.

A greater challenge was presented by the outbreak of war against Revolutionary France, the beginning of a period of hostilities that was to have enormous consequences for Britain. In June 1794 the Thirty-third sailed for the Netherlands to participate in the campaign already in progress, as part of the British contingent of an Allied army engaged against the French. Having pledged himself to Catherine Pakenham despite her family's disapproval, the twenty-four-year-old Wesley embarked on active service for the first time. It was an unfortunate campaign. Frederick, Duke of York, commanded the British force, leading troops in action for the first time in his life at the age of thirty-one. The army was beset by incompetence and disorganization, with a collapse in what passed for a system of supply, so that the troops were short of both food and warm clothing in a severe winter. It provided Wesley with his first experience of war, notably in a skirmish at Boxtel on September 15, 1794, his baptism of fire, in which he acquitted himself with a modicum of distinction. Despite his youth, he was not the most inexperienced commanding officer present, and at one period he appears to have had temporary command of a brigade of three battalions.

The campaign was a failure and the army had to retire into Hanover and from there returned to Britain (Wesley in March 1795). It was a salutory experience that emphatically demonstrated to him the importance of logistics, the necessity of keeping an army supplied and fed, and concern for the health of the ordinary soldiers. He believed that they were not to blame, remarking in later life that "I learnt more by seeing our own faults, and the defects of our system in the campaign of Holland, than anywhere else. . . . The infantry regiments, taken individually, were as good in proper hands as they are now, but the system was wretched";[6] and that "I learnt what one ought not to do, and that is always something."[7] Many of the failings he identified could have been remedied by an assiduous general; he claimed that between October 1794 and January 1795 his command received only one visit from a general belonging to the army's headquarters, only some twenty-five miles distant. This taught him never to make that mistake: "The real reason I succeeded in my own campaigns is because I was always on the spot—I saw everything, and did everything for myself." [8]

Following the Netherlands campaign, Arthur Wesley was frustrated in his attempts to secure further advancement. His family staunchly supported the Tory administration that held office, with but a brief hiatus, from the advent of William Pitt the Younger in 1783 until 1830, but despite the progress of his brother Richard in government service, influence and patronage were not sufficient to secure Arthur any further post. On May 3, 1796, he purchased another step in rank, to colonel, and when the Thirty-third was ordered to India, it was to that part of the burgeoning British empire that he directed his course.

At the time there existed no official establishment for the training of officers, let alone a staff college to impart the higher knowledge of the profession. Officers were expected to pick up what they needed once they had joined their regiments. Most would have received the general education expected of a gentleman, but even during the later stages of the Napoleonic Wars it was not impossible to find unit commanders ignorant of even the rudiments of drill, and some must have resembled one of the British army's most celebrated battalion commanders, "Mad John" Browne, of whom it was said that he only ever had one book, and that was the Army List. Arthur Wesley, however, was different. He was intent on improving his abilities, and as a colleague recalled him remarking, "he had always made it a rule to study by himself for some hours every day; and alluded to his having continued to act upon it." [9] Accordingly, he took a considerable library to India, many volumes on military theory and others concerned with the history, nature, and languages of the subcontinent. He also brought with him works of the philosophers John Locke and William Paley and the statesman Henry St. John, Viscount Bolingbroke; Sir William Blackstone's great commentaries on the laws of England; Adam Smith's *Wealth of Nations;* and a few of lighter vein, such as the works of Jonathan Swift, Voltaire's fables, and Rousseau's 1760 novel, *Julie, ou la Nouvelle Héloïse.*

The predominantly serious nature of Wesley's library might suggest that the young colonel was a dry and studious individual, but evidently that was not the case. George Elers, a fellow officer who met Arthur in September 1796, described him as "all life and spirits." He recorded that

> in height he was about 5 feet 7 inches, with a long, pale face, a remarkably large aquiline nose, a clear blue eye, and the blackest beard I ever saw. He was remarkably clean in his person, and I have known him shave twice in one day, which I believe was his constant practice.... He spoke at this time remarkably quickly, with, I think, a very, very slight lisp. He had a particular way, when pleased, of pursing up his mouth. I have often observed it when he has been thinking abstractedly.[10]

It was the serious study of his profession, however, that prepared him for the first great test of his military career.

Sepoy General

ALTHOUGH THE first British settlement in India dated
from the second decade of the seventeenth century, when Wesley
arrived at Calcutta in February 1797 British rule covered only a
portion of the subcontinent. Since the British presence originated
from commercial motives, a mercantile organization, the Honourable
East India Company, represented most of the British interest. Much
more than just a trading concern, it assumed the rights of virtually a
sovereign state, administering the government and maintaining an
army in each of the three British coastal settlements or "presidencies":
Bombay, Calcutta, and Madras. Its forces included some regiments
of Europeans, but the majority of the regiments were composed of
Indians who had been trained in European tactics and were commanded by British officers. The Indian troops were known as sepoys
(from the Hindustani word *sipahi,* a soldier) and the British officers
who led them might be termed—sometimes with a hint of dispar-
agement—"sepoy officers." From the mid-eighteenth century a small
number of "king's regiments"—units of the British army—were sent
to India to bolster the Company's forces, hence the arrival in India
of Wesley's Thirty-third. Each of the presidencies had a governor,

and in 1774 the first governor-general was appointed by a British Act of Parliament that gave the British government nominal ascendancy in governance. The incumbent of this office at the time of Wesley's arrival was Sir John Shore, later first Baron Teignmouth, whose resignation enabled the previous governor-general, Lord Cornwallis, to be reappointed; but he was occupied by the suppression of the 1798 rebellion in Ireland, and instead the newly appointed governor of Madras was advanced to the post of governor-general. For Arthur Wesley, who might otherwise have had to anticipate some years of fairly humdrum existence as a regimental officer, this appointment was crucial: the new governor-general was his elder brother Richard, Lord Mornington.

It was inevitable that Mornington's arrival in India would exert an influence on his brother's career, and this even included a change of name. As head of the family, Mornington decided that their name should revert to its older spelling, so in May 1798 Arthur adopted the name "Wellesley."

The expansion of British interests in India was less a matter of conquest than a process of alliance with compliant local rulers against those who had proved obstructive. Chief among the latter at the time was the ruler of Mysore, Tipu (or Tippoo) Sultan. Mysore had been hostile to the Company for years, from the time of Tipu's father, the great Hyder Ali, who had died in 1782. The last hostilities—the Third Mysore war—had ended in 1792, but as Tipu was canvassing French support, the British decided to eradicate the influence of their European enemy in the subcontinent by making a renewed effort against Mysore. The army was to be commanded by Gen. George Harris—for whom Wellesley had little affection—and included a substantial contingent provided by a local ally, the Nizam of Hyderabad. Having originally been appointed to organize logistical support—a task in which his painstaking methods proved invaluable and gave an early indication of his appreciation that supplies were the most important feature of an army—Arthur Wellesley was effectively given command of the Nizam's column (nominally led by the Nizam's chief minister). It included troops from Hyderabad, Company battalions from Madras and Bengal, and the

Thirty-third. The appointment of the governor-general's brother was regarded by some as sheer nepotism, and Maj. Gen. David Baird, who had a much smaller command, was especially resentful; having endured an appalling captivity in Mysore during the previous war, he had more reasons than most to seek the eradication of Tipu.

As Harris's army marched on Tipu's capital of Seringapatam, on March 27, 1799, it encountered a strong Mysorian force at Malavelly, east of the city; Tipu's army was forced to retreat in an action in which Wellesley's Thirty-third performed with especial credit. The army moved on to besiege Seringapatam, and on the night of April 5, Wellesley was ordered to make an attack upon the outlying village of Sultanpettah and the adjoining grove, the Sultanpettah Tope, using the Thirty-third with two Madras battalions in support. Nocturnal operations were notoriously difficult; the attack faltered amid the confusion of dykes and bamboo groves and the soldiers withdrew in confusion. Having led the advance, Wellesley went directly to Harris to report his failure in person; the general recorded that "Colonel Wellesley came to my tent in a good deal of agitation, to say he had not carried the tope . . . it must be particularly unpleasant to him."[1] It appears that Wellesley then fell asleep on a table, probably worn out by the effort.

The incident led to aspersions against his reputation. Two officers of the Twelfth Foot, a regiment involved in the adjoining operation against Sultanpettah, were notably critical, but both were very junior in rank and must have been recording secondhand camp gossip. Richard Bayly, one of those officers, claimed that Wellesley's actions "were those of a madman, rolling backwards and forwards along the long table," in tears and exclaiming, "My God, I'm ruined forever." Bayly stated that many thought that Wellesley should have been court-martialed if only "to clear his character from the odious stigma of cowardice, which was the prevailing opinion attached to his conduct by the whole army," but believed that General Harris did not have the nerve to criticize the governor-general's brother. "Here, as in every other situation of English society, the influence of aristocratic ascendancy manifested itself most powerfully," and in consequence of being denied an opportunity to vindicate his conduct, "Colonel Wellesley was left to the indiscriminate ordeal of public opinion. I know many old officers who declared they would never speak to him again, except in an official capacity."[2] George Elers was less critical but still believed that Wellesley escaped censure because he "was brother to the Governor-General of India, and that was enough to wipe away any neglect or bad management, if any existed; but I believe did not exist, and might have happened to any man, however experienced and vigilant."[3]

The consequences of Wellesley's reverse in the minor action at Sultanpettah demonstrated that despite the great advantages conferred by his family's position and connections, those very associations attracted criticism from some quarters, something that was to recur at other stages of his career. If there were any truth in Bayly's story, it was probably the only time in his military career that Wellesley gave way to despair and self-doubt; however, the action at Sultanpettah did have an effect on him, leaving him with an aversion to operations that lacked thorough reconnaissance and reinforcing his desire for personal control over all aspects of his forces.

Seringapatam was stormed on May 4 and Tipu was killed. Although he had played no part in the assault, Wellesley was appointed to administer the captured city. Although he was probably the officer best suited for the job, the appointment again gave rise to charges of nepotism and infuriated General Baird, who believed that he should have been given the command. Indeed, such were his objections that General Harris had to inform him that "an officer who thinks himself authorised to remonstrate with his superior can never be usefully employed,"[4] whereupon Baird backed down. In reward for Tipu's defeat, on December 2, 1799, Arthur's brother Richard was granted the title Marquess Wellesley.

Once established as an officer capable of exercising more than a battalion command, Arthur Wellesley was given increasing responsibility. In 1800 he led an expedition against a formidable bandit, Doondiah Waugh (or Wao). With a force of Indian troops and four king's regiments, Wellesley pursued and engaged Doondiah at Conaghull on September 10; though outnumbered at least two to one, Wellesley attacked immediately and routed the enemy.

Doondiah was killed; Wellesley then provided funds for the maintenance of the bandit's young son, who had been captured. On April
29, 1802, Arthur was promoted to major-general. Subsequent operations cemented Wellesley's reputation as a commander of stature.
Civil war among the Marathas, one of the most formidable of the
Indian powers, had led to the deposition of the British-supported
ruler, Peshwa Baji Rao II. The governor-general decided to support
the Peshwa, and in the resulting Second Maratha War of 1803–5,
Arthur Wellesley was entrusted with command of one of the British
operational columns; Gen. Gerard Lake commanded the other.

In May 1803 Wellesley restored the Peshwa to his capital, Poona,
without opposition, and some months of negotiation with the leaders of the Maratha Confederacy followed. Invested with political
authority, Wellesley undertook both diplomatic and military duties, a dual task he would perform in much of his subsequent career.
In the military sphere, his Indian service had emphasized the necessity of caring for the well-being of his troops and that proper supply
was as important as tactical genius. His orders demonstrated his
concern; an order from June 1803, for example, was typical.

> I do not wish you to issue flour to the sepoys; in fact it would not be
> cheaper than half a seer of rice: it introduces a new practice into the
> service, which is bad if it is not necessary; and as every change of
> food causes sickness, it may be prejudicial to their health.[5]

Also typical was his habit of supervising even minor concerns, and
the issue of precise instructions: "[G]ive directions that 2000 more
coolies loaded with rice may be sent to camp. An hircarrah and one
or two sepoys ought to come with each party, in order to keep them
together and show them the road."[6] In the tactical sphere, his Indian service demonstrated the importance of aggression, which together with their superior discipline enabled the small European
forces to engage and defeat the huge indigenous armies. Wellesley
commented on this in a letter to a subordinate in 1803:

> [T]he best thing you can do is . . . dash at the first party that comes
> into your neighbour hood. . . . If you succeed in cutting up, or in

driving to a distance, one good party, the campaign will be our own.
A long defensive war will ruin us.[7]

Diplomacy having failed to resolve the impasse with the Maratha leaders, Wellesley wrote to the most intractable, Doulut Rao Scindia, "I offered you peace on terms of equality, and honorable to all parties; you have chosen war, and are responsible for all consequences."[8] These consequences were immediate; two days later Wellesley broke camp and advanced on, and captured, the Maratha fortress of Ahmednuggur. On September 23, 1803, he engaged a huge Maratha army at Assaye; unlike some Indian armies, those of the Marathas included a nucleus of troops trained by European officers in European tactics. Though massively outnumbered—Wellesley had only some 7,000 troops, of whom 1,500 were British—he determined to attack without hesitation. The resulting victory was hardly a tactical triumph, but was won by hard fighting and discipline in which, presaging future actions, the British infantry stood like a red wall as their opponents crashed around them. Wellesley was himself in the thick of the fighting, losing two horses that day, and his casualties were heavy: 1,584 against perhaps 6,000 Maratha casualties. He admitted, "I should not like to see again such a loss as I sustained on the 23rd September, even if attended by such a gain."[9] Many years later, when asked what he considered to be his best action, he said simply, "Assaye."

Further victories followed, including the rout of Scindia's army at Argaum (November 29, 1803), in which Wellesley's forces suffered only minimal casualties, and on December 15 he captured the fortress of Gawilghur. These, with the successes of Lake's column, effectively confirmed the defeat of the Marathas, although hostilities continued until 1805. In these Wellesley took no part; indeed, he was somewhat dismayed at the conduct of the diplomacy. He was suffering from rheumatism, and with his brother due to be replaced as governor-general, there was a possibility that he might not find favor with the successor. He wrote, "I have served as long in India as any man ought, who can serve any where else; and I think that there appears a prospect of service in Europe, in which I should be more likely to get forward."[10] Ambition was not his only reason for wishing to leave the subcontinent; he was also homesick. He wrote of his anxiety to see his friends, and that even if he had no employment in Britain, no appointment would induce him to remain in India. In March 1805 he sailed for home.

India, however, had made him. In 1838 he claimed that on his return, "I understood as much of military matters as I have ever done since or do now."[11] That may have been an exaggeration, but Indian service undoubtedly refined his skills, both military and political, spheres that were often intertwined, so that diplomatic skills were needed to obtain the best from sometimes lukewarm allies and to maintain the confidence of his political masters. In the realm of diplomacy India was so instructive that he seems to have compared subsequent problems with those he had encountered in India, even on one occasion describing the great French statesman Talleyrand as resembling one of Scindia's diplomats—only less clever. Fair treatment and the observance of local customs were used to encourage cooperation from the Indian potentates; Jasper Nicholls, who served in the Maratha War, stated that he achieved this by

> promises, kindnesses, presents, indeed, by every kind of liberality of which he possessed the means . . . to the cutwahl he gave a heavy pair of gold bangles, of which he considerably advanced the value by putting them on his wrists with his own hands.[12]

Such practices brought forth expressions like that from the inhabitants of Seringapatam such as one in July 1804: "We have felt, even during your absence, in the midst of battle and of victory, that your care for our prosperity had been extended to us in as ample a manner as if no other object had occupied your mind."[13] Even in an age when fulsome tributes were not uncommon, the sincerity of this and subsequent expressions of regard seem genuine. Unlike many in India, however, Wellesley demanded scrupulous honesty; on one occasion when a huge sum was offered in return for a favor, he castigated the officer who reported it for not informing the prince concerned that any true British officer would regard it as an attempted bribe and an insult.

In the military sphere, although Wellesley would already have had an intimate knowledge of tactics, the Indian experience was most beneficial in acquiring the ability to manage a campaign, and certain aspects of his style of command were already evident. He realized that the maintenance of discipline was crucial, on the battlefield and off, the latter significant in not alienating local populations who might provide supplies: "If my Mahratta [*sic*] allies did not know that I should hang any one that might be found plundering . . . I should have starved long ago."[14] Such rigid enforcement of good order would be a feature of all his campaigns. An adequate system of supply was also essential; George Elers recalled that even early in Wellesley's time in India, he "was particularly severe upon any neglect of the commissariat department, and openly declared that, if he commanded an army, he should not hesitate to hang a Commissary for any dereliction of duty."[15]

India also established his fortune; with prize money and a reward for his services from the Company, he remarked that although not rich in comparison to others, he was when compared to his former situation, and that this "rendered me independent of all office or employment."[16] A further reward was a knighthood of the Order of the Bath, at that time the principal award for military achievement, and much more exclusive than it would be after its enlargement in 1815. From September 1, 1804, he was known as "Sir Arthur."

Despite some infirmities arising from the climate, in general Wellesley enjoyed the robust good health that he was to retain throughout his military career; as he remarked, he was never confined to bed and "never unable any one day to do whatever duty there happened to be before me."[17] Much of his good health was owing to his generally abstemious habits: eating plain food, drinking alcohol only in moderation, and taking regular exercise, all very different from some of the practices of the period. George Elers recalled that he

> kept a plain but good table. He had a very good appetite, and his favourite dish was a roast saddle of mutton and salad. . . . He was

very abstemious with wine; drank four or five glasses with people at dinner, and about a pint of claret after. He was very even in his temper, laughing and joking with those he liked, speaking in his quick way.[18]

These habits produced the stamina to rise early, ride long distances in his quest for personal reconnaissance—to be "always on the spot and see everything for myself"—and to retain clarity of thought heedless of fatigue. Indeed, when questioned subsequently about his great physical endurance, Wellesley remarked, "Ah, that is all India. India effected a total change in my constitution."[19]

Home, Denmark, and Portugal

S IR ARTHUR'S constitution was not the only thing enhanced by his seven years in India. He returned home with a reputation, although not one as marked as his military achievements might have justified; until the middle of the nineteenth century, commanders who had served in India—"sepoy generals"—were not regarded as highly as those who had forged a reputation in Europe. He returned to a nation still at war with France, now represented by Napoleon Bonaparte, who had secured his appointment to supreme power as Emperor of the French. The brief Peace of Amiens had broken down, and hostilities had recommenced. With his close connections with the governing ministry, Sir Arthur gave them the benefit of his opinions—direct and unvarnished—including to William Pitt, recently returned as prime minister, and to Lord Castlereagh, secretary of state for war and the colonies, who from 1812 directed British foreign policy. (Pitt was said to have remarked that Wellesley was unlike any other soldier he knew, in answering questions directly and always giving sound reasons for his opinions.) The connection with the ministry was of obvious benefit to the advancement of Wellesley's career, but he had less influence with the head of the army: he was never a favorite of Frederick, Duke of York, who held the post of commander-in-chief until his death in 1827 (minus a period of forced resignation in 1809–11 arising from a scandal involving his ex-mistress).

Wellesley was given command of a brigade for an expedition to north Germany, as part of the Allied strategy to defeat Napoleon, but Napoleon's crushing defeat of the Russo-Austrian army at Austerlitz on December 2, 1805, caused the expedition to be withdrawn. Instead, Wellesley received command of a brigade stationed at Hastings, on the southern coast of England, which might have been a crucial location had not Napoleon called off his intended invasion of England some time before. When asked how an officer of his distinction (albeit in the east) could accept such relatively lowly posts, Wellesley returned a characteristic answer.

> For this plain reason: I am nimmukwallah, as we say in the East; that is, I have ate of the King's salt, and, therefore, I conceive it to be my duty to serve with unhesitating zeal and cheerfulness, when and wherever the King or his government may think proper to employ me.[1]

In an age when matters of precedence and personal honor exercised the minds of many, this was a fairly remarkable statement.

Another duty awaited Wellesley on his return to England. He had never been immune to female charms, which indeed had been the cause of gossip in India. George Elers, for example, recalled that "Colonel Wellesley had at that time a very susceptible heart, particularly towards, I am sorry to say, married ladies," and that his aide-de-camp (ADC), Captain West of the Thirty-third, considered such behavior "highly immoral and indecorous, and a coolness took place between West and the Colonel."[2] Now, following his earlier courtship, he proposed to Kitty Pakenham. There is no evidence of pressure upon him to honor his earlier declaration of regard, and his motivation may have been partially from a sense of obligation, but in later years he admitted to his friend Harriet Arbuthnot that he had been a fool to honor his "understanding." In the decade since they had last met, they had had no direct correspondence, only the occasional communication via a mutual friend, and Kitty had not been without suitors (including Galbraith Lowry Cole, one of Wellesley's future divisional commanders), but now she was a thirty-four-year-old spinster whose looks were beginning to fade. They became engaged even before they met again, and when they did it was said that Wellesley muttered, "She has grown ugly, by jove!" but the veracity of this is uncertain.[3] They were married on April 10, 1806, in the Dublin home of Kitty's family. Although never desperately unhappy, it was never the most felicitous of unions; though Kitty was devoted to her new husband, she provided him with no intellectual stimulation and he was exasperated by her lack of care in financial and household concerns. The marriage was blessed by the birth of a son, Arthur Richard, on February 3, 1807, followed by Charles on January 16, 1808.

If military opportunities were limited, political ones were not, and on Castlereagh's advice Wellesley accepted the offer of a parliamentary seat, Rye, to which he was elected on April 1, 1806. His purpose was not to launch a political career—although at one time he considered it—but to assist the defense of his brother Richard, whose tenure as governor-general of India was being attacked. Richard's actions were vindicated, but the lobbying by his brothers on his behalf aroused resentment from those opposed to what was seen as a Wellesley clique. Sir Arthur found this period somewhat unpleasant in that the ministry he supported—the so-called Ministry of all the Talents, led by Baron Grenville—contained Whigs hostile to his brother, placing him in an uncomfortable position, alien to his more direct nature. In March 1807, however, the cabinet resigned over the king's refusal to accept Catholic emancipation, and the Duke of Portland became nominal head of a Tory administration, with Castlereagh as secretary for war. Sir Arthur—who had changed parliamentary seats, representing Mitchell, Cornwall, and from 1807 Newport, Isle of Wight, accepted the post of chief secretary for Ireland on April 3 under the new lord-lieutenant, the Duke of Richmond. On April 8, 1807, he was sworn in as a member of the Privy Council. He worked both in Ireland and at Westminster; in July 1807, for example, he obtained leave for a bill aimed at preventing insurrection in Ireland and introducing a scheme to register arms, which was the cause of "much accusation and recrimination between the leading Members on each side of the House, relative to the revival of religious animosity!"[4]

Military affairs, however, continued. On January 30, 1806, Wellesley had been appointed colonel of his old regiment, the Thirty-third, succeeding Cornwallis, which gave him much pleasure. He held the colonelcy until New Year's Day, 1813, when he took up that of the Royal Horse Guards, one of the most prestigious in the army. (Although colonel of the Thirty-third for less than six years, with his earlier command of the regiment it was sufficient for the regiment to be given his name after his death). In spring 1807 he informed Castlereagh that he wished to be part of an expedition being prepared for service in Europe, and that in any event he could not remain in his current position lest the army thought that he was using it to avoid military duties (evidently believing that part of the army establishment was suspicious of him on account of his political and aristocratic connections).

The expedition was to Denmark to coerce that nation into placing her fleet into British hands to keep it from Napoleon's grasp. Command was given to Lieutenant-General William, Baron Cathcart; Wellesley was allocated a divisional command. The campaign was not especially taxing, Danish military power being limited, though Wellesley won a sharp little action at Kjöge on August 29 for a trifling loss in which he handled his troops with the aggression learned in India. After a bombardment that caused considerable destruction in Copenhagen—which Wellesley disliked—the Danes surrendered. Wellesley drew up the articles of capitulation and signed them on Cathcart's behalf (September 7, 1807). A week later he applied for permission to return home, and since the position of chief secretary in Ireland remained open, he resumed his previous duties.

In addition to Irish duties, Wellesley served as unofficial military adviser to the ministry, notably to Castlereagh, and was given so much work that he remarked that he felt like a horse upon whose back anyone thought he had a right to put a saddle. Among the schemes under consideration was one advanced by the Venezuelan general Francisco Miranda, who proposed a campaign to free the South American colonies from Spanish rule. Wellesley was unenthusiastic; he stated later, "I always had a horror of revolutionising any country for a political object. I always said, if they rise of themselves, well and good, but do not stir them up; it is a fearful responsibility."[5] Nevertheless, having been promoted to the rank of lieutenant-general (April 25, 1808), Wellesley prepared to command a force assembling at Cork for an expedition to South America, but events in Europe intervened.

Having dealt with his opponents in Austria, Russia, and Prussia, Napoleon turned his attention toward the Iberian Peninsula. Pursuing his so-called Continental System, which aimed to close Europe to British trade, he sent an army through his ally, Spain, to occupy Portugal, which had refused to conform. Napoleon then engineered the abdication of King Charles IV of Spain and confined his son and legitimate successor, Ferdinand, Prince of the Asturias, under house arrest in France. Napoleon's brother, Joseph Bonaparte, replaced them as monarch of Spain. This caused widespread uprisings throughout the Peninsula, and local "juntas," or governments, were established to support the rightful king. The juntas appealed for assistance to the principal European power still at war with France: Britain. Wellesley advised that this presented a military opportunity, and the ministry was receptive to his opinion. In a notable speech on June 15, 1808, the foreign secretary, George Canning, declared that any nation opposed to France was thus an ally of Britain, and that nothing would serve British interests so well as a Spanish victory. It was decided that the expedition preparing at Cork should be sent to the Peninsula, and Wellesley was deputed to inform Miranda that the South American venture was called off. (He imparted this information when they were walking in the street, to prevent Miranda "bursting out."[6])

The prospect would have been daunting to some commanders, but Wellesley was confident in himself and in the troops he would lead. The record of the British army in recent campaigns had not been especially distinguished, but most of their disappointments had arisen from failings in command rather than in the system or in the regiments that composed it. With a capable commander, the army would prove a very different proposition.

Wellesley's confidence in his own ability was not shared by all those in authority, so when it was decided to increase the size of the expedition to the Peninsula, the choice for the commander of the reinforcement was Sir John Moore, Wellesley's senior. Moore was recognized as an officer of great merit but politically was not a "friend" of the administration, and the government seems to have been anxious that he should not enjoy overall command. Instead, they appointed Sir Hew Dalrymple, then-commander at Gibraltar, to be in supreme command, assisted by Sir Harry Burrard. Neither was inexperienced, but Dalrymple had seen no active service for some fifteen years, although in his post at Gibraltar he had established good relations with the Spanish. The cabinet seems to have hoped that Wellesley would distinguish himself sufficiently to assume command eventually, and Castlereagh wrote to Dalrymple:

> Permit me to recommend to your particular confidence Sir Arthur Wellesley. His high reputation in the service as an officer would in itself dispose you, I am persuaded, to select him for any service that required great prudence and temper, combined with much military experience. The degree, however, to which he has been for a length of time past in the closest habits of communication with His Majesty's Ministers . . . will, I am sure, point him out to you as an officer of whom it is desirable for you, on all accounts, to make the most prominent use which the rules of service will permit.[7]

Initially, however, Wellesley was on his own and indeed expressed a wish that he might defeat the French before the others arrived. His army, some 13,500 strong (his own troops from Cork plus a reinforcement under Sir Brent Spencer that had already been in Spain), disembarked in Portugal at Mondego Bay on August 1–5, 1808. The Portuguese royal family had fled to Brazil, but the governing council left behind was determined to resist the French occupation, and Wellesley made contact with the Portuguese forces already in the field. He spent his first days ashore organizing his commissariat, which, as throughout the Peninsular War, was dependent heavily on hired vehicles and teams taken from the countryside. Few had Wellesley's understanding of the importance of transport and supply, so the army's own transport organization was woefully insufficient. He also issued two characteristic documents. The first was a general order to his army emphasizing that the inhabitants of Portugal were allies and had to be treated with every courtesy, and their customs obeyed. The second document, a proclamation to the "People of Portugal," was published in conjunction with Sir Charles Cotton, the British naval commander in the region. The proclamation assured them that his troops landed "with every sentiment of friendship, faith, and honour," and that they were engaged in a struggle

> for all that is dear to man—the protection of your wives and children; the restoration of your lawful Prince; the independence, nay, the very existence of your kingdom; and for the preservation of your holy religion. . . . The noble struggle against the tyranny and usurpation of France will be jointly maintained by Portugal, Spain, and England.[8]

Wellesley commenced a march on Lisbon, which was occupied by the French army of Gen. Jean-Andoche Junot, an old friend of Napoleon's. Junot sent out forces to block his route, and on August 17, 1808, Wellesley mounted an attack against a French contingent under Gen. Henri-François Delaborde at Roliça.[9] Delaborde was forced to abandon his position but conducted a skillful withdrawal; the action was counted as Wellesley's first victory in the Peninsular War, but it was hardly an unqualified success. For that he had to wait a further four days.

More reinforcements arrived to bolster his small army, and with them came Sir Harry Burrard. Wellesley met him aboard ship and was told to curb his advance until Moore's larger reinforcement should arrive, Burrard being aware that the French strength in Portugal was greater than at first thought. Junot, however, intervened, attacking Wellesley's position at Vimeiro on August 21.[10] It was an example of what has become accepted as the classic Anglo-French Peninsular War confrontation (although this is a great oversimplification):

French attacks against British troops in a sound defensive position, or what Wellesley was later to describe as coming on in the old style and being beaten back in the old style. The French were beaten back and badly mauled, and Wellesley believed that the opportunity existed to increase the scale of this already considerable victory by advancing immediately upon Lisbon. Burrard, however, who had arrived in the middle of the battle and let Wellesley finish what he had begun, then assumed command and forbade any further advance. His caution may have been reasonable, but it infuriated Wellesley and probably the army as well. He was reported to have remarked "with a cold and contemptuous bitterness . . . 'You may think about dinner, for there is nothing more for soldiers to do this day.'"[11]

Worse was to follow. Dalrymple arrived the following day and supported Burrard in his caution. The opportunity to capture Lisbon while the French were disorganized was lost, and Wellesley found Dalrymple unreceptive to his advice and indeed believed that Dalrymple was deliberately prejudiced against him. Before the new British commander could make plans for the next stage of the campaign, the French sent an envoy under a flag of truce to discuss an armistice. From that developed the contentious Convention of Cintra, by which Junot undertook to evacuate all French troops from Portugal by sea, with all their equipment and "private property of every description," which in effect was all the loot they had accumulated.[12] In essence this accomplished the purpose of the British expedition, the removal of the enemy from Portugal, but the terms granted to the French caused an uproar at home: namely, that they were to be evacuated without being regarded as prisoners of war and thus were able to serve against Britain and her allies without restriction, and that they were permitted to carry off a vast quantity of plunder from an ally's territory. Wellesley added his name to the Convention—he claimed to have done so because Dalrymple asked him to, rather than from any belief in it—but almost immediately complained about it, not for its removal of the French (for the timidity of his superiors had lost the opportunity secured by Vimeiro) but for its generosity of terms, and implied further criticism by stating, "I do not know what Sir Hew Dalrymple proposes to do . . . but if I were in his situation I would have 20,000 men at Madrid in less than a month."[13]

Such was the outrage at the terms offered to Junot—notably in the press, and even William Wordsworth wrote a tract against the Convention—that the government had to order an official inquiry. All three senior British generals were recalled, leaving the British forces in the Peninsula in the hands of the newly arrived Sir John Moore. Sections of the British press attacked Wellesley for his influential family connections: the newspaper *The News*, for example, deplored his being given a dinner by the Duke of Richmond, stating that "every patriotic and honest heart in this empire felt almost as much indignation on reading this account of the dinner . . . as it did on reading the articles of the armistice which he signed and negociated" [*sic*], and suggested that if he were exonerated it would owe less to his innocence than to "the sinister efforts of his friends" at the expense of the other two "unbefriended" generals.[14] Convened on November 14 and delivering its verdict in the following month, the court of inquiry came to the conclusion that no action should be taken against the signatories, but it was clear that only Wellesley was exonerated fully. He had resumed his duties as chief secretary for Ireland but was present in the House of Commons on January 27, 1809, to receive a vote of thanks for his victory at Vimeiro.

Peninsula: The Defensive Phase

BY THE time Wellesley received his vote of thanks, the situation in the Iberian Peninsula had changed markedly. Determined to secure his brother's place on the throne of Spain, Napoleon had arrived there in person to crush Spanish resistance and had routed the Spanish armies that had opposed him. Sir John Moore led most of the British forces in Portugal in support of the Spanish but had to abandon his advance into Spain after Madrid surrendered to Napoleon with hardly any struggle. Moore, however, had succeeded in diverting Napoleon's attention from crushing Spanish resistance, since Napoleon used a considerable proportion of his forces to pursue Moore, who retreated toward the northwest coast of Spain. Believing his task largely completed, Napoleon left Spain in January 1809 while the drive against Moore continued; after a most arduous march, the British stood at bay at Corunna and defeated the pursuing French (January 16, 1809), and were evacuated by sea. Moore lost his life in the action. With a strong base established at Cadiz in southwest Spain, the fires of Spanish resistance to Napoleon continued to burn.

The officer who succeeded Moore to command the British presence that remained in Portugal, Sir John Cradock (later

"Caradoc," Lord Howden), was pessimistic about the prospect of resistance. On March 7, 1809, however, Wellesley submitted to the government a "Memorandum on the Defence of Portugal," which began with the statement:

> I have always been of the opinion that Portugal might be defended, whatever might be the result of the contest in Spain; and that in the mean time the measures adopted for the defence of Portugal would be highly useful to the Spaniards in their contest with the French.[1]

It was a clear, concise, and optimistic document that described in only a thousand words how the Portuguese military establishment could be revived by uniting British and Portuguese soldiers under British command with an enhanced British presence to fill the most severe deficiencies in the Portuguese army, notably in artillery, cavalry, light troops, and commissariat, the latter of crucial significance. Wellesley appreciated that it would be a considerable undertaking, especially financially, but argued that profound benefits could result. The argument was convincing: on April 6 he received the letter that appointed him to command the British forces in the Peninsula. Having resigned his post as Irish secretary and his parliamentary seat, he was in Lisbon only some sixteen days later.

The situation that greeted him was not auspicious. Although he had some 22,000 British troops, the Portuguese were not yet in a fit state to contend with such an excellent army as that of the French. Having already overrun northern Portugal, the French marshal Jean-de-Dieu Soult, one of Napoleon's most competent subordinates (who had supervised the final pursuit of Moore), was at Oporto with 20,000 men. Marshal Michel Ney with an equal number was further north in Galicia, and an even larger army under Marshal Claude Victor was in a position to invade central Portugal. Wellesley acted almost immediately; detaching troops to contain Victor, he moved on Oporto, where Soult believed himself secure behind the river Douro, having destroyed its bridges. This first operation conducted by Wellesley since his return to the Peninsula resulted in no major action but was a victory of maneuver: on May 12 he put troops across the river in boats and established a sufficiently robust bridgehead to resist French attempts to drive him back. Soult was compelled to abandon Oporto and began to retreat, and, as Wellesley pursued, was fortunate to escape with the loss of about one-quarter of his men and much of his baggage and artillery.

Two significant changes occurred before further operations were undertaken. On June 18—a date that would become indivisibly associated with him six years later—Wellesley instituted a divisional system within his British army. Hitherto, no larger organization than a brigade had existed, but by linking brigades into divisions the transmission of orders and supplies was facilitated, which was vital for the smooth running of the army and increasingly important as it increased in size. Initially Wellesley had only troops to create four infantry divisions; by March 1811 there would be eight. Secondly, on July 6, 1809, Wellesley was appointed marshal-general of Portugal. The Portuguese provisional government gave him complete command over their forces, so that British and Portuguese became integrated into a single army. The reconstruction of the Portuguese forces was entrusted to one of the most reliable of Wellesley's subordinates, William Beresford, who excelled in organizational tasks and who transformed the military establishment as marshal of the Portuguese army.

To combat the next most imminent French threat, Wellesley proposed to cooperate with the Spanish army of the captain-general of Estremadura, Gen. Gregorio de la Cuesta. The association was infelicitous from the beginning: old and infirm, Cuesta was obstructive, unwilling to cooperate or to release supplies to the British and was duly reviled by his allies. John Colborne, one of the most intelligent and capable British regimental officers, described him as "a perverse, stupid old block-head,"[2] and William Warre, a British officer attached to the Portuguese army, claimed he was an "obstinate surly old ignorant fellow . . . quite superannuated, and so violent and obstinate that everybody feared him but his enemies."[3]

Wellesley's joint operation plans were almost ruined by Cuesta's intransigence. Wellesley complained repeatedly to both the Spanish and British authorities, "[I]f the people of Spain are unwilling to supply what the army requires, I am afraid that they must do without its services," and threatened that "till I am supplied, I do not think it proper, and indeed I cannot, continue my operations in Spain."[4] Wellesley moved against the French army of King Joseph (which had incorporated Victor's corps, and had Marshal Jean-Baptiste Jourdan as its chief of staff), but was foiled in his attempt to bring it to battle by what he described as Cuesta's "whimsical perverseness of his disposition."[5] On July 27, 1809, British and Spanish armies concentrated to meet Joseph and Victor at Talavera de la Reina. The first French probe was greeted by a huge volley at impossibly long range by a section of Cuesta's force; Wellesley remarked that he hoped they would fire so well on the morrow, even though at that moment there was no one to shoot at. Then part of the Spanish line bolted, as if frightened by their own noise; it proved that despite the considerable martial qualities of the Spanish soldiers, at this stage of the war their leadership and training were such that little reliance could be placed on them.

On the following day Victor made his main attack on the British line; Cuesta's army was hardly engaged. Thanks to its steadiness, the British army just held firm, though it was a desperate fight: over the two days Wellesley lost some 5,367 men out of his total of 20,600, about 26 percent. French losses were heavier but represented a considerably smaller proportion of their army. The French retired and on the following day Wellesley reported that he intended to pursue "as soon as my troops are a little rested and refreshed, after two days of the hardest fighting I have ever been a party to. We shall certainly move towards Madrid, if not interrupted by some accident on our flank."[6] Shortly after, however, he was complaining bitterly about his allies, that

> our half starved army, which, although they have been engaged for two days, and have defeated twice their numbers, in the service of Spain, have not bread to eat. It is positively a fact that, during the last seven days, the British army have not received one third of their provisions; that at this moment there are nearly 4000 wounded

soldiers dying in the hospital in this town [Talavera] from want of common assistance and necessaries, which any other country in the world would have given even to its enemies; and that I can get no assistance of any description from the country. I cannot prevail upon them even to bury the dead carcasses in the neighbourhood, the stench of which will destroy themselves as well as us.[7]

There was no possibility of exploiting the victory of Talavera, for Wellesley had to turn away to deal with the threat to his flank, which he had predicted from a much-reinforced Soult, that compelled him to fall back on the Portuguese frontier. Cuesta abandoned the wounded who had been left behind in Spanish care; they were then captured by the French, to the fury of the British army. Wellesley was incensed and dismayed by the quality of the Spanish leaders and complained again of their lack of understanding of the crucial matter of supplies: "No troops can serve to any good purpose unless they are regularly fed; and it is an error to suppose that a Spaniard, or a man or animal of any country can make an exertion without food." He worried that "the army will be useless in Spain, and will be entirely lost, if this treatment is to continue."[8] He also wrote of the "miserable state of discipline" of the Spanish troops, "and their want of Officers properly qualified. These troops are entirely incapable of performing any manoeuvre, however simple."[9] He became convinced that at this stage cooperation with the Spanish was futile, and that he must henceforth reply upon his own resources and those of Portugal.

Talavera, however, had a lasting effect upon Wellesley's personal career: on August 26 it was announced that he had been ennobled with the title of Viscount Wellington of Talavera and Wellington. The choice of name was not his; since there was haste to reward him, his brother William had to choose the name. He selected "Wellington" from the town in Somerset, as being near to that of Wellesley. With commendable circumspection, Wellesley waited until he had seen the announcement in the official Gazette before he used his new signature on September 16, 1809, characteristically on a letter concerning commissariat matters, notably with regard to "some biscuit which was left by the British troops at Elvas last year." With a personal touch not usual in his very concise style of correspondence, he added as a postscript, "This is the first time I have signed my new name."[10]

It would be more than a year before Wellington, as he was now known, fought another major battle, but the intervening period would be as important as any during his period of command in the Peninsula. Having decided that it was impossible to rely on effective cooperation with the Spanish armies, the security of Portugal became paramount. The nature of its borders made a defense of the entire country unfeasible; but the key point was the capital, Lisbon, a port city, provided the seaborne link, protected by the Royal Navy, between the British forces and Britain itself and was the only factor that made the entire project sustainable. To secure this base, Wellington implemented perhaps the most important fortification to be created during the period.

In a letter of October 20, 1809, to the army's chief engineer, Sir Richard Fletcher, Wellington set out the design and purpose for the "Lines of Torres Vedras," named from one of its principal points. Lisbon's protection would involve a double line of fortifications running from the Atlantic to the Tagus estuary, consisting of some 152 mutually supportive strong points, and rendering the capital impregnable from an attack by land. Utilizing features of the terrain, the forts and defensive positions were constructed by a small staff of engineer officers and gangs of Portuguese peasants who performed the manual labor; they ranged from posts designed to accommodate fifty men and three nine-pounder guns to posts for 1,720 men and twenty-six guns. Fletcher's chief assistant, Maj. John Jones, described the project as "the foresight and skill of the general, and the exertion of the engineer . . . in happy unison."[11] By the time the lines were ready for occupation, even though the Portuguese civilians had been paid a fair wage, the entire work had cost less than £100,000, a remarkable example of efficiency.

The Lines of Torres Vedras were designed to be defended by some 18,000 Portuguese militia (14,000 for the inner line of fortifications). The main field army of regular troops was to remain in reserve behind them to oppose any breakthrough, but so well were the defenses organized that this was never a realistic possibility. For relatively small cost and minimal military effort, Wellington thus ensured the security of his base in the Peninsula, an impressive example of strategic foresight.

In the hiatus between major battles, Wellington remained busy, notably in improving the Portuguese army and integrating Portuguese brigades into British divisions to create a unified army. He introduced British officers into the Portuguese regiments at all levels until the caliber of the Portuguese military allowed Wellington to declare them "the fighting cocks of the army"; and characteristically added, given the importance he placed upon the delivery of supplies, "I believe we owe their merits to the care we have taken of their pockets and bellies than to the instruction we have given them."[12] Subsequently a Portuguese division was formed, but Wellington believed that the Portuguese were too reliant on a shared system of supply to function on their own. He successfully resisted a proposal that the Portuguese troops be concentrated into an independent army, stating that the existing system

> has answered admirably, has contributed in a principal degree to our great and astonishing success, and has enabled the Portuguese government and nation to render such services to the cause, and has raised their reputation to the point at which it now stands . . . if the Portuguese troops were separated from the British divisions . . . and they were not considered . . . part of ourselves, they could not keep the field in a respectable state.[13]

Political and diplomatic matters continued to occupy much of Wellington's attention in the relationships he developed with the governing bodies in Britain, Spain, and Portugal. There were ministerial changes at home; embarrassed by the failure of the expedition to Walcheren in the Netherlands, the Duke of Portland's administration gave way to that of Spencer Perceval. The Earl of Liverpool replaced Castlereagh as secretary for war and the colonies, but Wellington continued to enjoy a cordial relationship with the holder of this most important office and retained family influence in the government. The Marquess Wellesley served as foreign secretary until February 1812, and their younger brother Henry became ambassador to "free" Spain, a position he was to hold until 1822 and in which he was of great help to Wellington. In the absence of the Portuguese royal family, Wellington dealt with the ruling Council of Regency, headed by Jose Antonio de Menezes e Sousa, often referred to as "the Principal Sousa." Brother to both the prime minister of the royal family in Brazil, Rodrigo de Sousa Coutinho, Conde de Linares, and to the Portuguese ambassador in London, Domingos Antonio de Sousa Coutinho, later Conde de Funchal, was well placed to exert influence, though Wellington found him "weak rather than ill-intentioned." Another member of the Council, the Cardinal Patriarch of Lisbon, Antonio de Castro, late bishop of Oporto, he thought "a very bad fellow . . . no talent, only low cunning. He was a very unprincipled man . . . an old rogue," and claimed that both he and the Principal used to send him anonymous threatening letters.[14] The war minister Miguel Forjas he thought "a most able and well-meaning man . . . the ablest man I had to do with in the Peninsula."[15] In August 1810 Wellington himself became a member of the Council of Regency. Evidently never one to underestimate his own significance, on one occasion he criticized government attempts to influence his plan of operations, which "will end in forcing me to quit them, and then they will see how they will get on. They will then find that I alone keep things in their present state."[16]

Serious campaigning resumed in 1810 when Napoleon ordered one of his most capable marshals, André Massena, to recapture Portugal with resources that far outnumbered Wellington's army. Throughout the war, however, the number of troops Napoleon deployed in the Peninsula was less significant than the way in which the troops were deployed. To a certain extent Napoleon employed a policy of "divide and rule," so that each of his armies was virtually autonomous with its own commander; however, mutual jealously among such leaders hindered full cooperation to maximize the effect of their weight of numbers. Nevertheless, Massena's forces were formidable, as was his reputation, as Wellington himself testified:

"[T]he ablest, after Napoleon was, I think, Massena";[17] "I found him oftenest where I wished him not to be."[18] Nevertheless, when appointed to lead the French "Army of Portugal" in April 1810 Massena was possibly past his best, distracted by the presence of his mistress and afflicted by very bad relationships with his subordinates, which culminated in his dismissal of the respected Michel Ney for insubordination in March 1811.

The principal routes for the march of an army between Spain and Portugal were guarded by pairs of frontier fortresses: in the north, Almeida on the Portuguese side and Ciudad Rodrigo on the Spanish, and in the south the corresponding cities of Elvas and Badajoz. The French laid siege to the Spanish garrison of Ciudad Rodrigo in late April 1810 and battered it into surrender on July 9. They opened siege lines against Almeida on August 15, and after the its magazine exploded on August 26, the garrison surrendered on the following day. With the road into Portugal thus opened, Massena advanced down the valley of the Mondego, but Wellington blocked his route at a position of formidable strength at Busaco.

One of Wellington's greatest strengths as a defensive general was his ability to utilize the terrain to his advantage, Busaco being a classic example. He positioned his troops on a steep ridge, up which the French had to attack, and on September 27 they were repelled by the tactic that became a hallmark of Wellington's system. Despite a disparity in the numbers actually engaged—about 47,000 French to Wellington's 34,000, though the latter's total force was considerably larger—Massena was repelled with a loss of about 4,000 men to Wellington's 1,253. The French advance was not neutralized, however; they moved past the ridge and Wellington retired. His decision to fight at Busaco, he wrote,

> afforded me a favourable opportunity of showing the enemy the description of troops of which this army is composed . . . the Portuguese . . . have proved that the trouble which has been taken with them has not been thrown away, and that they are worthy of contending in the same ranks with the British troops in this interesting cause, which they afford the best hopes of saving.[19]

In October Wellington withdrew his troops behind the Lines of Torres Vedras to winter in safety. Massena's situation was very different: unaware of the existence of the Lines, he was astonished to find such an impregnable position, and what amounted to a "scorched-earth" policy had reduced the amount of food and forage available to the French in the countryside they occupied. Massena and his army sat outside the Lines all winter, never daring to attack, slowly starving, and weakening from disease and the activities of Portuguese irregulars. Finally, in March 1811, Massena was compelled to withdraw, abandoning much of his baggage and having lost perhaps 25,000 men during the campaign. The Lines of Torres Vedras had proved more costly to him, over a period, than any pitched battle. A number of sharp actions were fought as Wellington pursued, notably at Sabugal on April 3, 1811, when one of Wellington's most ineffective subordinates, Sir William Erskine, left the Light Division unsupported in an attack against a French force that outnumbered them greatly. The British success was a case of the excellence of the troops outweighing the deficiencies of command, upon which Wellington commented (with surprising diplomacy, given Erskine's failings), "Although the operations of the day were . . . not performed in the manner that I intended they should, I consider the action that was fought by the Light Division to be one of the most glorious that British troops were ever engaged in."[20]

The subsequent campaigning of 1811 revolved around the frontier fortresses. Badajoz had fallen in March to Marshal Soult, commanding the French "Army of the South," and as Wellington's most reliable deputy, Rowland Hill, was on leave, Marshal Beresford was entrusted with the operations against Badajoz, while Wellington himself concentrated on the more northern fortress of Almeida, now with a French garrison. Massena marched to their assistance and Wellington met him at Fuentes de Oñoro on May 3, 1811, when there was a preliminary engagement, followed by the main French assault on May 5. Again Wellington was outnumbered—some 37,500 men to 48,450 French—but Massena was defeated in a very hard-fought action, losing about 2,850 casualties to Wellington's 1,789. Reporting to Lord Liverpool, Wellington commented, "From the great superiority of force to which we have been opposed upon this occasion, your Lordship will judge of the conduct of the Officers and troops";[21] but privately admitted that it had so desperate an encounter that "if Boney had been there, we should have been beat."[22] It was Massena's last battle—Marshal Auguste-Frédéric Marmont replaced him on May 7—but the immediate aftermath was an embarrassment for Wellington. The French garrison at Almeida slipped away unopposed, thanks to Erskine's ineptitude, although blame was probably unjustly laid on Lt.-Col. Charles Bevan of the Fourth Foot. Bevan shot himself, and some blamed Wellington for the tragedy. Wellington complained of the quality of his assistants: "I am obliged to be everywhere and if absent from any operation something goes wrong."[23] The Almeida episode so tarnished a hard-won victory that the government decided not to ask for a parliamentary vote of thanks, to which Wellington agreed, remarking to Liverpool,

> [Y]ou acted right in not proposing a vote in Parliament on the battle of Fuentes. The business would have been different if we had caught the garrison of Almeida . . . people in England appear to me to be so much elated by any success, and so much depressed by any temporary check, that I feel difficulty in describing the state of our affairs.[24]

Meanwhile, Soult was intent on relieving Badajoz, which Beresford had begun to besiege. He turned to meet Soult's advance and on May 16 the armies clashed at Albuera in one of the bloodiest actions of the war. Although a fine administrator, Beresford was undistinguished in independent field command, and his victory at Albuera was attributable more to the courage of his troops and the initiative of subordinates than to any great ability on his part. After the battle, he wrote a rather despairing report to Wellington. Wellington's own dispatches were generally concise and as accurate as possible in the immediate aftermath of an action—in the accuracy of casualty-returns at least he attempted to present the unvarnished truth to his political masters and, as they were always published, to the public—but he was always conscious of the need to retain support for the war. Later he recalled the receipt of Beresford's first account of Albuera:

> He wrote me to the effect that he was delighted I was coming; that he could not stand the slaughter about him nor the vast responsibility. His letter was quite in a desponding tone. It was brought to me next day . . . and I said directly, "This won't do; write me down a victory." The dispatch was altered accordingly.[25]

Even so, he wrote a kindly note of reassurance to Beresford that contained an element of his military philosophy: "You could not be successful in such an action without a large loss, and we must make up our minds to affairs of this kind sometimes, or give up the game."[26] The real consequences could not be concealed, however, and three days later he noted, "The late action has made a terrible hole in our ranks; but I am working hard to set all to rights again."[27] On May 27 Wellington took over Beresford's force, which henceforth became the main field army.

Following Albuera the siege of Badajoz was renewed, but Wellington abandoned it on June 10 after two assaults on outworks were beaten back; shortages in siege artillery and engineers proved fatal. Marshal Marmont, a friend of Napoleon's but not as effective as Massena in his heyday, advanced to relieve Wellington's blockade of Ciudad Rodrigo. Sir Thomas Picton's Third Division fought a sharp action that beat back a French thrust at El Bodon (September 23), while Hill surprised and defeated a French division at Arroyo dos Molinos (October 28), but the year ended with the great frontier fortresses of Badajoz and Ciudad Rodrigo still in French hands.

The year 1811 was not the most successful in terms of decisive victories, but it could be said to mark the end of Wellington's defensive phase of the Peninsular War. Portugal was secured and the French attacks on it repelled, while in southern Spain Cadiz successfully resisted a long French siege. The British forces deployed in that part of the Peninsula were also nominally under Wellington's control, and the third largely British victory of the year had occurred on

March 5, when Marshal Victor attacked an Anglo-Spanish army as it marched along the coast road toward Cadiz. The British contingent, led by the elderly Scottish general Sir Thomas Graham, was left to fight virtually unaided and at Barossa won a victory at heavy cost. Graham was so critical of his Spanish allies that he would have found it impossible to work with them as head of an independent British force, so he transferred to Wellington's army, where he became a valued subordinate. From the turn of the year 1811 into 1812 the focus of Wellington's operations became more offensive than defensive, as his strength increased and the war began to swing against the French. It was also from this period that Napoleon began to withdraw troops from Spain to participate in the invasion of Russia in 1812 and the campaign in Germany that followed the debacle of the retreat from Moscow.

Wellington: The Man and the General

AT THIS stage it is appropriate to consider some of the traits and abilities that defined Arthur Wellesley both as an individual and as a military commander. An early appreciation was published late in 1810:

> Lord Wellington is about four and forty years of age, rather tall and thin, of a fine countenance and piercing eye. He rises every morning at three o'clock, breakfasts at four, and always, before day-light, visits the grand battery of Sombral, upon which are mounted ninety pieces of cannon. His Lordship then returns to his tent, and writes his letters, &c. which done, he mounts his horse, and rides along the line, about twenty miles, sees that everything goes well, provides for the comfort of the soldiers, and cheers them in their duty. Returning to his tent, he dines, surrounded by his officers; always frank, affable, cheerful, and full of anecdote, he makes them forget their fatigues, while he endears them to their General, and himself to them. Between nine and ten at night, his Lordship lays himself down in his clothes, as do all the officers, and at three in the morning he is up again. His thin habit is believed to be partly owing to fatigue of body and mind. His ardent spirit supports him.[1]

As this suggests, there was almost a hint of asceticism in his personal habits, at least in comparison with some others of the period. The Earl of Ellesmere remarked that although "no man's valet had less to do in the way of personal attendance [his] dress was scrupulously neat . . . his ablutions were not of the partial and scanty old school. He not only looked clean, but was so."[2] Contrasting with the elaborate uniforms favored by some generals, on campaign Wellington wore almost civilian dress, commonly a low cocked hat with waterproof cover and a plain blue or gray frock coat. George Gleig, who went out to the Peninsula as a seventeen-year-old subaltern, recalled his first sight of Wellington, an entirely typical impression:

> A thin, well-made man. . . . His dress was a plain grey frock, buttoned to the chin; a cocked-hat, covered with oilskin; grey pantaloons, boots, buckled at the side; and a steel-mounted light sabre. Though I knew not who he was, there was a brightness in his eye which bespoke him something more than an aide-de-camp or a general of brigade. . . . There was in his general aspect nothing indicative of a life spent in hardships and fatigues; nor any expression of care or anxiety in his countenance. On the contrary, his cheek, though bronzed with frequent exposure to the sun, had on it the ruddy hue of health, while a smile of satisfaction played about his mouth, and told, more plainly than words could have spoken, how perfectly he felt himself at his ease.[3]

Wellington's lack of interest in the minutiae of regulation uniform was reflected in his attitude to his troops. His concentration was entirely on practicalities; commenting on a proposed alteration of the army's uniform in 1811, he wrote that

> there is no subject of which I understand so little; and, abstractedly, speaking, I think it is indifferent how a soldier is clothed, providing it is in a uniform manner; and that he is forced to keep himself clean and smart, as a soldier ought to be. But there is one thing I deprecate, and that is any imitation of the French, in any manner. It is impossible to form an idea of the inconvenience and injury which result from having any thing like them, either on horseback or on

foot. . . . At a distance, or in action, colours are nothing; the profile, and shape of a man's cap, and his general appearance, are what guide us. . . . The narrow top caps of our infantry, as opposed to their broad top caps, are a great advantage to those who are to look at long lines of posts opposed to each other.[4]

This utterly practical view was clearly appreciated, as noted by William Grattan, an officer of the Eighty-eighth Foot:

Lord Wellington was a most indulgent commander; he never harassed us with reviews, or petty annoyances, which so far from promoting discipline, or doing us good in any way, have a contrary effect. . . . Provided we brought our men into the field well appointed, and with sixty rounds of good ammunition each, he never looked to see whether their trousers were black, blue or grey; and as to ourselves, we might be rigged out in all the colours of the rainbow if we fancied it.[5]

To this insistence on practicality Wellington added his own industry. He was a tireless worker, and though he did devote some time to recreation while in the Peninsula—notably hunting—it never intruded on his duty. Throughout his life he maintained an astonishing capacity for correspondence, notably to subordinates and political masters, issuing precise directives to the former and providing unvarnished accounts to the latter. His dispatches are models of clarity and emphasize not only breadth of vision but the care he took over the most minor details. The volume of his correspondence was huge but never neglected, his rule being "to do the business of the day in the day." Nothing that might affect the smooth running of his army was too small a concern. For example, when William Kelly of the Fortieth Foot eloped with a Portuguese girl in 1813, Wellington wrote, "I beg that you call upon Lieut. Kelly to restore the young lady to her family. . . . I cannot allow any officer of this army to be guilty of such a breach of the laws of Portugal."[6]

A further proof of his industry was his habit of being "always on the spot," seeing and doing everything for himself. An indefatigable horseman, he expected his staff to keep up with a punishing schedule. His friend and Spanish liaison officer at headquarters, Gen. Miguel Alava, told how he would always ask Wellington when they would start the next day and what they might expect for dinner; the reply was usually the same, and Alava admitted that he came to regard with horror the words "at daylight" and "cold meat." [7]

Although Wellington was in complete command of the military forces under his jurisdiction, without having to consult his political masters on the everyday planning of operations but only on wider aspects of policy (though having to be sufficiently diplomatic to maximize the cooperation of his allies), there were aspects in which he was not in complete control. One of the most significant was in the appointment of subordinates. He could express a preference for a certain officer—he asked for Sir Thomas Picton, for example, "a rough foul-mouthed devil as ever lived, but he always behaved extremely well; no man could do better in the different services I assigned to him"—but the ultimate decision rested with the commander-in-chief, who from 1809 to 1811 was Sir David Dundas and thereafter the Duke of York. [8] Wellington's relationship with the army establishment was sometimes strained, though he took a pragmatic attitude to the influence of patronage, stating on one occasion that promotion entirely upon merit would have been desirable, but that it was inevitable that the commander-in-chief and his associates would have friends and relations for whom they would seek employment, and so he had to make the best of the situation. Even after all his success, as late as May 1815 he had to complain:

> I might have expected that the Generals and Staff formed by me in the last war would have been allowed to come to me again; but instead of that, I am overloaded with people I have never seen before; and it appears to be purposely intended to keep those out of my way whom I wished to have. [9]

As a consequence, Wellington was allocated subordinates neither competent nor to his liking. The problem was exacerbated by contemporary etiquette: no general officer could be expected to serve under one of equal rank who was junior in terms of seniority, so a valuable officer might be lost if a senior officer arrived and had to have a command found for him. An example was Wellington's problem with the excellent Robert Craufurd, who had asked for leave; Wellington told him,

> Adverting to the number of General Officers senior to you in the army, it has not been an easy task to keep you in your command; and if you should go, I fear that I should not be able to appoint you to it again, or to one that would be so agreeable to you, or in which you could be so useful.[10]

The existence of the Portuguese army solved one such problem: when Wellington finally found an officer of talent to lead the artillery, Lt.-Col. Alexander Dickson, he was appointed by virtue of his Portuguese commission. He would have been ineligible had his British rank been the only criterion, since he was junior to other British artillery officers.

Being bound by the prevailing system of etiquette and anxious not to alienate the military establishment at home, Wellington rarely felt able to dismiss or demand the recall of those whose appointment owed more to patronage than ability, even if their presence was detrimental to the army. He did, however, manage to weed out some of the least useful by less than outright dismissal. For example, in December 1811 he wrote to Henry Torrens, the commander-in-chief's military secretary, that in regard to general officers, "we have now more than we can well dispose of," and that there were two "with whom we could dispose with advantage . . . respectable officers as commanders of regiments, but they are neither of them very fit to take charge of a large body." One, he reported, "wishes to return home, to unite himself with a lady of easy virtue," and that the other had been ill, so "I shall try if I can to get them away in this manner, as I would not on any account hurt the feelings of either."[11]

It might seem unusual that the smooth running of an army could be jeopardized by the acceptance of unsuitable senior officers so as not to offend them, but it was the accepted practice. In consequence, Wellington was encumbered by some who were almost a menace.

An example was Sir William Erskine—the officer responsible for the Almeida disaster—whose appointment Wellington queried on the grounds that it was thought that Erskine was insane. Torrens's reply can hardly have dispelled his doubts: that certainly Erskine was a little mad, but was uncommonly clever when lucid, and that it was hoped that he would have no fit during the campaign, even though he had appeared "a little wild" when he embarked! (Poor Erskine evidently did have a fit: he died in 1813 after jumping from a window).

Contemporary mores also deprived Wellington of the services of perhaps the most outstanding British cavalry leader of his generation, Henry William Paget, Earl of Uxbridge (and subsequently Marquess of Anglesey). He had proved his abilities in Moore's Corunna campaign but could not be appointed to serve under Wellington until 1815 for family reasons; Paget had eloped with the wife of Wellington's brother Henry.

Wellington could be criticized for giving even his most trusted subordinates too little opportunity to exercise their initiative and develop their skills in semi-independent command. There is some truth in that criticism, but with some of even the most well-meaning subordinates having only limited ability, it is hardly surprising that Wellington was unwilling to hazard the success of the campaign by delegating too much responsibility to someone who was unable to handle it. While the army was relatively small, it was possible for him to oversee most of the important concerns in person (and many of minor significance), but as it became larger and began operating over greater distances, he was compelled to delegate some responsibility for field command. He had a small number of very reliable assistants, notably Rowland Hill and to a lesser extent William Beresford and Thomas Graham, who acted almost as corps commanders (though in the Peninsula there was never officially any organization larger than a division). Wellington's own opinion seemed to favor Beresford, "the ablest man I have yet seen with the army," and his own thoughts on the qualities required of a commander were expressed when some of his generals asked him who should succeed him if he were to be killed or incapacitated.

Again he chose Beresford, saying, "If it was a question of handling troops some of you fellows might do as well, nay, better than he; but what we want now is some one to feed our troops, and I know no one fitter for the purpose than Beresford."[12] Again, Wellington's concern for the regular supply of his troops was paramount.

Wellington's relationships with his senior subordinates seem to have been based on the etiquette of good manners and an unwillingness to hurt their feelings, and with some he enjoyed genuinely warm relations. He wrote to Hill's nephew after that general's death in 1842 that "nothing ever occurred to interrupt for one moment the friendly and intimate relations between us,"[13] though perhaps this was influenced by the fact that, as Wellington commented, "Hill does what he is told."[14] Conversely, his censure of those who blundered could be cutting. An example concerned Robert Craufurd, alias "Black Bob," the taciturn but indomitable commander of the Light Division, who tarried too long in withdrawing his command after he received his orders, content that he could defend his position. According to Judge-Advocate Francis Larpent, "Lord Welling-ton, when he came back, only said, 'I am glad to see you safe, Craufurd.' To which the latter replied, 'Oh, I was in no danger, I assure you.' 'But I was, from your conduct,' said Lord Wellington. Upon which Craufurd observed, 'He is d—— crusty to-day.'"[15] On occasion, Wellington seems to have believed that a more severe reprimand could be counterproductive, but at other times his anger could be volcanic. One instance occurred after Salamanca when the head of the medical department, the great humanitarian Sir James McGrigor, reported that he had diverted commissariat resources from the route Wellington had planned. This produced a furious outburst: "Who is to command the army? I or you? . . . As long as you live, sir, never do so again; never do anything without my orders."[16] So violent was this reaction that it astonished the artist Francisco Goya, for whom Wellington was sitting at that moment. But while he was capable of reducing a subordinate to tears, the heat of his rage soon cooled, as in this case when he promptly invited McGrigor to dinner.

The appointment of unwanted and unsuitable subordinates was not the only interference with which Wellington had to contend. A problem of some duration was the Duke of York's insistence on re-calling battalions that had become reduced in numbers and replac-ing them with full-strength but raw units from home. Of this Wellington disapproved strongly, remarking that the presence of seasoned campaigners was invaluable: "It is better for the service here to have one soldier or officer . . . who has served one or two campaigns, than it is to have two or even three who have not."[17] His practical solution was to amalgamate two weakened units into a "Provisional Battalion," thus maintaining a workable tactical entity without losing the battle-hardened men, but this ongoing struggle with the army command at home resulted in the loss of some of his prized veterans. It must have been with considerable irony that, as field commander, he wrote in April 1812 to Lord Liverpool, and mentioning the Duke of York, "Your Lordship and His Royal High-ness are the best judges of what description of troops it is expedient that this army should be composed."[18]

Another example of necessary deference to the influence of the commander-in-chief concerned the appointment of what amounted to a new chief of staff. In Wellington's headquarters no such post was nominated officially, administrative functions being divided between the departments of the Quartermaster-General and Adjutant-General. By virtue of his ability, the head of the former, Sir George Murray, had come to resemble a de facto chief of staff, but he applied for home leave in late 1811 and was replaced by James Willoughby Gordon, a great favorite of the Duke of York. Gordon attempted to reform the administrative system of the head-quarters staff, creating a poisonous atmosphere, and was clearly in-competent (on one occasion a junior officer overheard a private shout-ing match between him and Wellington). Even worse was Gordon's leaking of confidential matters to his friends in the parliamentary opposition at home. Wellington was apparently unwilling to dis-miss him after only a short period, as this would have been an affront to the Duke of York. Gordon himself eventually solved the difficulty by going home to receive treatment for a painful medical condition, and subsequently the admirable Murray returned to the position.

As a general, Wellington possessed every necessary skill, from the ability to discern the enemy's intentions and reacting accordingly to the handling of troops in battle. In the former, one officer commented that even had the French army "been in the bowels of the earth Lord Wellington would have found them out."[19] Wellington was effectively his own head of intelligence, collating the reports of a network of agents and highly skilled "observing officers" who operated behind enemy lines, and in Sir George Scovell had the services of a skilled code breaker (who unraveled the "great Paris cipher" used by the French so that Wellington could understand captured documents). As Wellington once expressed it, he always tried to discover what lay "on the other side of the hill" and used an interesting comparison to describe his system of operations. His French opponents, he said,

> planned their campaigns just as you might make a splendid set of harness. It looks very well; and answers very well; until it gets broken; and then you are done for. Now I made my campaigns of ropes. If anything went wrong, I tied a knot; and went on.[20]

Although in extreme circumstances his troops might go unfed for days together, in general his recognition of the importance of the delivery of supplies enabled him to concentrate his forces when required and not rely (as to a considerable extent did the French) on the troops' ability to forage for themselves, and thus the strategic maneuver of his army was not so dependent on its ability to feed itself.

As a tactician, Wellington developed no very radical system but instead utilized the prevalent practices. One factor, however, characterized his handling of troops: the "reverse slope" deployment used in the Peninsular War and at Waterloo. Much has been made of the supposed superiority of the British line formation over the French attack in column, but to reduce this to a mathematical calculation of the number of muskets that each formation could bring to bear is to underestimate its significance.

French tactics, as developed from the early Revolutionary Wars, often relied on the speed and cohesion of an infantry advance against the enemy, either to batter through their line or for the column to deploy into line at musket range to maximize its own firepower, and for such advances to be preceded by a horde of skirmishers to harass the enemy by sharpshooting and to conceal the main body. This tactic had proved successful against a number of continental enemies, but the counter Wellington employed proved crucial. In his Peninsular army, light infantry tactics formed a vital cog in the machine: the light companies of the various battalions were supplemented by companies of skirmishers generally deployed at brigade level, including some armed with rifled muskets of much greater accuracy than the smooth-bored firearms carried by the rest (and almost exclusively by the French). This enabled each of Wellington's formations effectively to counter the French skirmishers.

Wellington's favored tactic was to hold high ground where his troops could be deployed on a "reverse slope," behind the crest of a ridge, up the forward slope of which the French would have to advance. Only Wellington's skirmishers would be thrown forward and visible to the enemy; his main body would thus be protected from the enemy's fire, and with its position unknown, the French would not be able to judge the correct moment for deploying from column to line (if such deployment were the intention, which does not always seem to have been the case). The classic confrontation proceeded thus: when the French columns approached the crest of the ridge, the British skirmishers would fall back as the main infantry line advanced to the crest, surprising the French by their appearance and unnerving them by their absolute silence (the French customarily advanced with much noise and shouting). The British would then deliver a crushing volley of musketry, which would devastate the head of the French column, and while the remainder were in confusion, the British would cheer and attack with the bayonet. The French could not resist and would retire in disarray, tumbling back down the hill; after a short pursuit the British would halt, reform, and return to their original position to await another attack, which could be repelled in the same manner. The above is a great simplification (many Peninsular actions could not follow this course owing to the nature of the terrain), but its essence was the classic Wellingtonian tactic. The excellence of Wellington's infantry contributed in a large portion to this success, as he recognized: on the eve of the Waterloo campaign he was asked what he thought would be the decisive factor in the coming conflict, whereupon he pointed to a British infantryman and remarked, "There, it all depends upon that article whether we do the business or not. Give me enough of it, and I am sure."[21]

Wellington relied less upon his other "arms of service." He never had artillery in sufficient quantity to use it as an offensive weapon but distributed it throughout the army in what was basically a supporting role. He was less successful in handling cavalry, in part because of a perceived lack of discipline among the troops and (primarily) their officers, who tended to sacrifice order for celerity and dash. Wellington's cavalry fought a number of outstanding actions but was always more of a support arm, or one to exploit a success already set in motion by the infantry, rather than a principal offensive force.

A criticism that could be leveled against Wellington was that he was predominantly a defensive general. From the beginning of his Peninsular career caution was rather forced on him in that he realized that the force under his command was the principal field army that the country possessed. As he admitted in 1813, he could not

> afford, or the British government or nation would allow of my being as prodigal of men as every French general is . . . we have but one army, and . . . the same men who fought at Vimeiro and Talavera fought the other day at Sorauren . . . if I am to preserve the army, I must proceed with caution.[22]

This led to Wellington being compared to the Roman general Quintus Fabius Maximus, known as "Cunctator" ("the delayer"); but Wellington was only defensive when circumstances dictated and could act offensively—notably at Salamanca, for example—when conditions were suitable. Even within a "defensive" battle he could act offensively and always seemed to be on hand at whichever point seemed most at risk. The Chamberlain of the Corporation of the City of London delivered a reasonably fair assessment in a speech given when Wellington was granted the Freedom of the City of London in July 1814: "A more illustrious instance is not recorded in history, of the caution of Fabius, most happily combined with the celerity of Caesar."[23]

Another factor contributed toward the excellence of Wellington's army: the ordinary soldiers' confidence in him. His relationship with them, however, was much different from that pertaining to Britain's earlier great military commander, the Duke of Marlborough, or that between Napoleon and his followers, both of whom at times were viewed with something between reverence and idolatry. Wellington became increasingly popular with the ordinary soldiers as they experienced the management of his campaigns and his habit of victory, but he was never taken to their hearts in the way that Marlborough was known to his men as "Corporal John."

Perhaps the most famous of all Wellington's statements is his description of the ordinary British soldier as "the scum of the earth." This might be interpreted as evidence of patrician contempt for social inferiors, but although Wellington used the expression on more than one occasion, this was not the case. Perhaps most notably he used it in a discussion comparing the French system of conscription with the voluntary enlistment by which the British army was recruited and which generally involved only the lowest levels of society:

> The conscription calls out a share of every class—no matter whether your son or my son—all must march; but our friends [the ordinary British soldiers] are the very scum of the earth. People talk of their enlisting from their fine military feeling—all stuff—no such thing. Some of our men enlist from having got bastard children—some for minor offences—many more for drink; but you can hardly conceive such a set brought together, and it is really wonderful that we should have made them the fine fellows they are.[24]

On at least one other occasion he made the same comparison, so that while the remark did arise originally from his own social position,

it was surely not intended to be dismissive of those who marched in his army.

Nevertheless, Wellington always maintained an aloof bearing toward those not in his immediate circle, especially toward the enlisted men, but this was not at all unusual at the time; indeed, officers who attempted to ingratiate themselves with the ordinary soldiers were reduced in the estimation of the latter, who expected their leaders to be superior to them in the social hierarchy. Benjamin Harris, who produced one of the most memorable contemporary accounts by an ordinary soldier, remarked that the rank and file responded best to an officer with "authority in his face," while an officer recalled his own sergeant lamenting the officer's departure: "I said, 'You have got a smart officer, Mr. B . . . , to look after you all.' 'Yes Sir,' he replied, 'but he is not a gentleman.'"[25] It is against this background that Wellington's attitude to his ordinary soldiers should be considered.

That attitude varied according to circumstance. When he passed the Thirty-third Foot at a fairly crucial stage of the battle of Waterloo, a veteran who had served with him in India called out, "Let us have three cheers for our old Colonel," but Wellington just held up his telescope and said, "Hush, hush, hush," as if fearful that any outburst of emotion would disorder the ranks.[26] Conversely, on a rather less desperate occasion in the Peninsula, a regiment heralded his approach by calling, "Douro! Douro!" (a name derived from his first title of nobility); he responded by removing his hat and bowing to them. Not on every occasion could he keep his emotions in check; it was reported that when the wounded in a field hospital raised three cheers for him in 1812, he turned away, covering tears with his handkerchief.

This is not to say, of course, that Wellington did not hold the prejudices associated with his aristocratic background. Among his most insensitive statements was that "I have never known officers raised from the ranks turn out well, nor the system answer; they cannot stand drink."[27] Although this was inaccurate, such views would not have been thought exceptional by the standards of the time.

Early in his Peninsular War career, Wellington did not command the universal respect of his army. An example is a published comment

by an anonymous officer who criticized Wellington's perceived failings in the operations before Talavera when he believed the general was "dreaming of something else" rather concentrating on the campaign:

> To account for these things in a man of Sir Arthur's reputation, is impossible. Some have asked, Who lost Mark Anthony the world?— A female (one, I believe, the mistress of Soult, and captured at Oporto), accompanies the head-quarter establishment. She has not a handsome face, but a good figure, and sits astride on horseback as knowingly and neatly as Mister Buckle himself.[28]

Statements of this nature led Wellington to complain about the amount of ill-informed comment that found its way from the army to the press at home.

After some experience of campaigning, however, the army came to regard Wellington with almost universal trust. He was seen as a commander who would do everything possible to keep them fed, would not risk their lives unnecessarily, and who would ensure success. He was nicknamed "Hooky" or "Beaky" (from his facial features) and one officer overheard a soldier use a concise and accurate description of him as "that long-nosed beggar that licks the French."[29]

John Kincaid, an officer in the Ninety-fifth Rifles, articulated what must have been a widespread appreciation:

> He was not only the head of the army but was obliged to descend to the responsibility of every department in it. In the different branches of their various duties, he received the officers in charge, as ignorant as schoolboys, and, by his energy and unwearied perseverance, he made them what they became—the most renowned army that Europe ever saw. Whenever he went at its head, glory followed its steps—wherever he was not—I will not say disgrace, but something akin to it ensued. . . . Lord Wellington appeared to us never to leave anything to chance. However desperate the undertaking—whether suffering under momentary defeat, or imprudently hurried on by partial success—we ever felt confident that a redeeming power was

at hand, nor were we ever deceived. Those only, too, who have served under such a master-mind and one of inferior calibre can appreciate the difference in a physical as well as a moral point of view—for when in the presence of the enemy, under him, we were never deprived of our personal comforts until prudence rendered it necessary, and they were always restored to us again at the earliest possible moment.[30]

In terms of the army's morale, this confidence in a commander was invaluable, and was recorded by many contemporary writers. George Gleig of the Eighty-fifth remarked, for example, that

> I felt, as I gazed upon him, that an army under his command could not be beaten; and I had frequent opportunities afterwards of perceiving how far such a feeling goes towards preventing a defeat. Let troops only place perfect confidence in him who leads them, and the sight of him, at the most trying moment, is worth a fresh brigade.[31]

John Bainbrigge of the Twentieth remembered how, after a rough day in the Pyrenees where Wellington had not been present initially, "I can never forget the joy which beamed in every countenance when his Lordship's presence became known; it diffused a general feeling of confidence through the ranks."[32] Kincaid again recalled how

> [W]e would rather see his long nose in the fight than a reinforcement of ten thousand men any day. . . . I'll venture to say that there was not a bosom in that army that did not beat more lightly, when we heard the joyful news of his arrival.[33]

More prosaically, John Cooper of the Seventh Fusiliers remembered how, as he and his comrades advanced into an inferno of shot at Albuera, when under Beresford's command, his friend, Fusilier Horsefall, "drily said, 'Whore's ar Arthur?' meaning Wellington. I said, 'I don't know, I don't see him.' He rejoined, 'Aw wish he wor here.' So did I." [34]

Peninsula: The Offensive Phase

Having secured the frontiers of Portugal, and with the pendulum of supremacy beginning to swing away from the French, Wellington prepared to take the offensive for the campaigning year of 1812. In his way stood the great border fortresses of Ciudad Rodrigo and Badajoz, which could not be safely bypassed if his army were to enter Spain, but the military authorities at home had left him woefully short of the wherewithal to prosecute sieges, notably in an entirely inadequate force of engineers. The historian William Napier, who saw the problem firsthand, recorded this:

> To the discredit of the English government, no army was ever so ill provided with the means of prosecuting such enterprises [sieges]. The engineer officers were exceedingly zealous . . . but the ablest trembled when reflecting upon the utter destitution of all that belonged to real service . . . the best officers and the finest soldiers were obliged to sacrifice themselves in a lamentable manner. . . . The sieges carried on in Spain were a succession of butcheries, because the commonest resources of their art were denied to the engineers.[1]

It is against this background and Wellington's inability to improve the situation, that the sieges of 1812 should be regarded.

Nevertheless, the siege of Ciudad Rodrigo commenced on January 8, 1812, and it was stormed and captured on January 19. Casualties were quite heavy and the city was looted after the storm, a precursor to future events. Among the casualties was Robert Craufurd, commander of the Light Division, who was mortally wounded in the attack; before he died he expressed regret that there should ever have been a difference between himself and Wellington, who recalled that "Craufurd talked to me as they do in a novel."[2] In recognition of the capture of the city, the Spanish Regency awarded Wellington the title of Duque de Ciudad Rodrigo, and on February 18, 1812, he was advanced in the British peerage to an earldom.

Badajoz proved a tougher prospect; the first siege trenches were opened on March 17 and the city was stormed on the night of April 6–7. It was one of the bloodiest events of the entire period; breaches in the outer wall were stormed repeatedly without success but at appalling cost of life, "as respectable representation of hell itself as fire, and sword, and human sacrifice could make it," according to Kincaid.[3] Wellington considered abandoning the assault, until a diversionary attack by escalade gained entry. After a fierce fight the French governor withdrew to an outlying fortification and surrendered the next morning. Despite the surrender, there occurred such an orgy of pillage and brutality that brought nothing but shame upon the victorious army: William Grattan of the Eighty-eighth stated that every infamy that humanity could devise was perpetrated. Losses had been heavy (in the entire siege Wellington had suffered at least 1,035 killed and more than 2,100 wounded, including 800 dead in the storming), but not even such trauma could excuse the collapse of discipline and the brutality that followed. Many witnesses wrote of their horror and disgust at this stain on the army's reputation, and Wellington must have had it in mind when he reported some two months later that "the outrages committed by the British soldiers belonging to this army, have become so enormous" that they risked alienating the local population, which should have been allies.[4] Wellington finally quelled the rampage by moving in fresh troops and erecting a gallows as a threat. He reported the action to Lord Liverpool in one of his regular dispatches, noting, "It is impossible that any expressions of mine can convey to your Lordship the sense which I entertain of the gallantry of the officers and troops upon this occasion," which was certainly a justified comment, but privately he was appalled by both the disorder and the slaughter.[5] Later he admitted that he was in tears when Picton came to see him and was ashamed that he should be seen in such an emotional state. The iron-willed Picton was amazed at the display, and Wellington tried to cover his inner turmoil by cursing the government for not providing adequate resources.

There occurred a significant change in the personnel of the government following the assassination of Spencer Perceval, the prime minister, on May 11, 1812; Liverpool became prime minister and was succeeded by Earl Bathurst as secretary for war, while earlier Castlereagh had replaced Richard Wellesley as foreign secretary. The changes did not affect the determination to prosecute the war, and Wellington prepared for its next stage. He faced the threat of two French armies (the French command was still not unified): Marshal Soult in the south and Marshal Marmont in the north. He detached Hill to observe Soult and marched against Marmont, entering the great city of Salamanca and beginning the siege of the surrounding forts on June 17, 1812. Three days later, Marmont's army skirmished with Wellington's outposts, but the French withdrew as Wellington probed forward and on June 27 the Salamanca forts surrendered. On July 3 Wellington commented that he thought a battle was not imminent, as "Marmont will not risk an action unless he should have an advantage; and I shall certainly not risk one unless I should have an advantage"; but on July 22 the armies came into contact near Salamanca in terrain dominated by the heights of the Greater and Lesser Arapiles.[6] As Wellington reported,

> Marmont . . . after manoeuvering all the morning in the usual French style, nobody knew with what object, he at last pressed upon my right in such a manner, at the same time without engaging, that he would have either carried our Arapiles, or he would have confined us entirely to our position. This was not to be endured, and we fell

on him, turning his left flank; and I never saw an army receive such a beating.[7]

There are several accounts of how Wellington took the initiative at what was perhaps the most pivotal moment of his Peninsular campaigning. He lunched on a chicken leg while observing the French maneuvering, and discerned through his telescope how the enemy formations had become strung out. Traditionally he exclaimed either, "By God, that will do," or "By God, they are extending"; mounted and dashed to a better vantage point; and turning to his friend the Spanish liason officer, said, "Mon cher Alava, Marmont est perdu" (My dear Alava, Marmont is lost). In a style that perhaps demonstrates how Wellington was regarded by his army, William Napier described how Wellington had observed the flaw in the French maneuvers:

> The fault was flagrant, and he fixed it with the stroke of a thunderbolt. A few orders issued from his lips like the incantations of a wizard, and suddenly the dark mass of troops which covered the English Arapiles, was seemingly possessed by some mighty spirit, and rushing violently down the interior slope of the mountain, entered the great basin amidst a storm of bullets which seemed to sheer away the whole surface of the earth. [8]

Among the orders Wellington issued were those to his brother-in-law, Edward Pakenham, temporarily commanding the Third Division: "Ned, d'ye see those fellows on the hill? Throw your division into column; at them! and drive them to the devil."[9] Pakenham, evidently a more emotional man than Wellington, solemnly shook hands before he got his command moving; Wellington gave him his hand, "but with no relaxation from his usual rigidity. Even under such circumstances anything like display of sentiment was uncongenial to him."[10] Subsequently Wellington commended Pakenham:

> [H]e made the manoeuvre which led to our success in the battle of the 22nd, with a celerity and accuracy of which I doubt that many are capable, and without both it would not have answered its end.

Pakenham may not be the brightest genius, but my partiality for him does not lead me astray when I tell you he is one of the best we have.[11]

The grasping of this opportunity—which one present exemplified by stating that "Lord Wellington, with the eye of an eagle, and the rapidity of lightning, changed his defence into an attack"—dispels the notion that Wellington was entirely a defensive general.[12] Marmont was wounded in the action, as was his immediate successor in command, and the French army was swept away in disorder. The victory would have been greater had not the Spanish general Carlos de España evacuated Alba de Tormes and, as Wellington wrote, "was afraid to let me know that he had done so. . . . If I had known there had been no garrison at Alba, I should have marched there, and should probably have had the whole."[13] Nevertheless, though neither truly decisive nor one of the bloodiest of the war (Marmont lost some 14,000 men, Wellington about 5,200), Salamanca virtually ensured that the French could not win the war from that stage.

In recognition of the victory, Wellington was advanced another step in the peerage to marquess (August 18, 1812). Only six days later he was complaining that "I have been going on for more than three years upon the usual allowance of a Commander in Chief, that is ten pounds per diem, liable to various deductions, among others of income tax, reducing it to about eight guineas." But as he had so many expenses, he had to plead for an increase,

or I shall be ruined. . . . I believe there is no service in which a Commander in Chief, with such a charge as I have, is so badly paid. . . . I should not have mentioned the subject, knowing that the public expect in these days to be well served at the lowest possible rate of expense, if I did not find that I was in a situation in which I must incur expenses which I cannot defray without doing myself an injury.[14]

On August 12 Wellington entered Madrid amid scenes of wild rejoicing, but the next stage of his operations was a severe reverse.

Despite the lack of suitable resources he laid siege to the town of Burgos, held by a French garrison with an energetic commander, Gen. Jean-Louis Dubreton. From September 19 until the siege was abandoned on October 21–22, unsuccessful attempts were made at its capture at considerable cost. To Liverpool, Wellington explained that he had had insufficient transport to move his artillery and munitions to Burgos. He mentioned the failure of a subordinate to carry out his instructions but admitted that the failure was ultimately his: "The Government had nothing to say to the siege. It was entirely my own act."[15] Years later, he acknowledged:

> It was all my own fault; I had got, with small means, into the forts near Salamanca. The Castle was not unlike a hill-fort in India, and I had got into a good many of those. I could get into this, and I very nearly did it, but it was defended by a very clever fellow. . . . As fast as I established myself, he attacked and drove me out.[16]

Worse was to follow. Wellington has been criticized for not pursuing the French after Salamanca, but confident of taking Burgos, he had even hoped that "before Christmas, if affairs turn out as they ought, and Boney requires all the reinforcements in the North, to have all the gentlemen safe on the other side of the Ebro,"[17] implying the ejection of the French from western and southern Spain. Instead, the approach of strong French forces necessitated a very damaging and dispiriting retreat from Burgos, and on November 1 the French reoccupied Madrid. On the day before that Wellington admitted, "I have got clear, in a handsome manner, of the worst scrape I ever was in," but recent events had caused some dismay within the army.[18] Following the breakdown of discipline during the retreat, Wellington issued a circular admonishing officers for not attending to their duty, an unjust criticism that was resented, and one junior officer wrote home to say that the war was lost and that Wellington had ruined himself by acting like a madman. By the spring, however, a much more senior officer reported that the Burgos debacle had had no lasting effect, that the army still regarded

Wellington as a peerless idol, and for him they would offer their lives as willingly as they would drink his health.[19]

In September 1812 the Spanish government had appointed Wellington as generalissimo of their armies, which position the Prince Regent had granted him permission to accept on October 21. This position gave him supreme command over the entire Allied war effort throughout the Peninsula, but it also caused a number of problems: Gen. Francisco Ballesteros, one of the most active of the Spanish commanders, was so vociferous in his protests against Wellington's appointment that he was arrested and removed from command. Leadership of the Spanish forces was to bring Wellington many headaches, for as with his own government he found that political interference detracted from his ability to maximize the military effort. In November 1812, for example, one of his regular complaints about the administration and political direction of the Spanish authorities claimed that without improvements "it is quite hopeless to continue the contest in the Peninsula with the view of obliging the French to evacuate it by force of arms,"[20] and a cause of particular irritation was the removal from his command, for political reasons, of the most successful Spanish general of the war, Francisco Castaños, in June 1813. Wellington described this decision as "harsh and unjust," but he was unable to dispute it.[21]

In December 1812 Wellington received a vote of thanks in parliament for Salamanca, although an implacable opponent of the ministry, Sir Francis Burdett, commented that it was an inferior victory to Marlborough's triumph at Blenheim and that success was as remote as ever. Parliament also awarded a sum of £100,000 to permit Wellington to purchase an estate.

The army recuperated and increased in strength during the winter of 1812–13, and the spring brought the beginning of the final drive to victory in the Peninsula. As Wellington's resources increased, those of the French decreased as Napoleon recalled elements to help replace the losses of his disastrous Russian campaign; Soult was among those sent for. As the 1813 campaign began Wellington crossed the frontier from Portugal on May 22, and it was reported that he doffed his hat and declared, "Farewell, Portugal! I shall never see you again."

Wellington in the uniform of a major general in India, 1804. *Print after Robert Home*

Wellington at Conaghull in India on September 10, 1800. *Engraving by J. Rogers after Abraham Cooper*

Wellington's older brother Richard, Marquess Wellesley. *Engraving by Hunt after Sir Thomas Lawrence*

Wellington's first French opponent on the Peninsula, Gen. Jean-Andoche Junot, Duc d'Abrantes. *Engraving by T. Read*

Joseph Bonaparte, King of Spain. *Engraving by Mauduison*

Frederick Augustus, Duke of York, commander-in-chief of the British Army in 1795–1809 and 1811–27. *Engraving by Skelton after Sir William Beechey*

Types of Wellington's soldiers during the Peninsular War (from left): Fourth (King's Own) Regiment of Foot; First (Royal) Dragoons; Highland Regiment. *Engraving published by T. Goddard and J. Booth*

A medallion by George Mills commemorating Wellington's victory at Talavera, produced by James Mudie some years later (Wellington being shown in the uniform of a field marshal).

One of Wellington's most formidable adversaries, Marshal André Massena, Duc de Rivoli, Prince d'Essling. *Print after Bonne-Maison*

A scene from the Battle of Busaco shows a typical Wellingtonian tactic, the defeat of French columns by British line. *Print by C. Turner after Maj. Thomas S. St. Clair*

A medallion by Thomas Halliday commemorating Wellington's victories from Assaye to Badajoz.

A medallion designed by Nicholas Brenet commemorating Wellington's entry into Madrid following the Battle of Salamanca.

Marshal Jean-de-Dieu Soult, Duc de Dalmatie, Wellington's opponent in the Pyrenees. *Engraving by E. Findon after H. Grevedon*

Wellington as a field marshal, 1814. *W. Say after Thomas Phillips*

Wellington attired as he was at Waterloo. *Tietze after Sir Thomas Lawrence*

Emperor Napoleon, defeated by the combined efforts of Wellington and Blücher at Waterloo. *Engraving by J. François after Paul Delaroche*

Wellington and his staff at Waterloo. *Engraving by S. Mitan after Capt. George Jones*

Wellington (right center) at Waterloo, alongside the Earl of Uxbridge. *Engraving by Freeman after W. H. Brooke*

"Stand up, Guards!" Wellington prepares the Foot Guards to repel the final French attack at Waterloo. *Engraving by S. Mitan after Capt. George Jones*

With his staff at Waterloo, directing the advance after the repulse of the last French attack. *Print published by R. Bowyer, 1816*

The meeting of Wellington and Blücher at La Belle Alliance at the end of the Battle of Waterloo. *Engraving published by Thomas Kelly, 1817.*

Wellington writing his Waterloo dispatch while his aide, Sir Alexander Gordon, lies mortally wounded in the next room. *Engraving after Lady Burghersh*

Wellington circa 1820. *Sir Thomas Lawrence*

In middle age, in his usual unostentatious civilian attire. *Unsigned 1830 print*

In old age, from an 1853 print. *G. Baxter*

The room in Walmer Castle in which Wellington died, including his simple camp bed. *Contemporary watercolor by R. T. Landells*

Wellington's funeral carriage. *Contemporary engraving*

His subsequent maneuvers continually got the better of his opponents, the principal French army in his path being commanded, at least in name, by King Joseph, with Marshal Jean-Baptiste Jourdan as his assistant. The French blew up the fortifications of Burgos rather than sustain a second siege, and on June 21, 1813, Joseph and Jourdan were engaged at Vitoria. Wellington's tactics—an offensive on two fronts—produced a victory so comprehensive that the French abandoned not only their baggage but all but two of their guns, one of which was lost two days later. The strategic consequence of the victory was huge: the French hold on Spain, weakened by Salamanca, was irredeemably broken. Among the trophies sent back to Britain was Jourdan's baton, the symbol of his appointment as a Marshal of France; by return, the Prince Regent sent to Wellington the baton of a field marshal of Britain, a promotion to the highest rank in the army that was backdated to the day of Vitoria.

On July 12, 1813, Soult took over command of the French forces in Spain from King Joseph, who Napoleon effectively dismissed despite his regal status. Soult's recall to the Peninsula thus placed all French forces under unified command for the first time (excepting the army of Marshal Louis-Gabriel Suchet in Catalonia and Aragon), but too late to affect the outcome of the war. All that Soult could hope to do was to hold the line of the Pyrenees to prevent an invasion of southern France, with the fortresses of San Sebastian and Pamplona acting as bastions for that line. This was Wellington's next objective, and ever mindful of the importance of his logistics, he switched his main base from Lisbon to the port of Santander on the north coast of Spain, from which the French had been expelled, which radically shortened his line of communications.

Soult was not content to act entirely upon the defensive but made attacks upon the advancing Allied troops as they entered the Pyrenees, achieving local superiority in numbers on more than one occasion. Some of the hardest fighting of the war occurred there, notably at Roncesvalles and Maya (July 25, 1813) and Sorauren (July 28–30); Soult initially achieved some success but was defeated heavily. Wellington commented that

I never saw such fighting as we have had here. It began on the 25th, and, excepting the 29th, when not a shot was fired, we had it every day till the 2nd. The battle of the 28th was fair bludgeon work.[22]

Both the great border fortresses were besieged and, after one failed attempt in July, abandoned because of the French offensive. San Sebastian was captured by assault on August 31, the garrison of its citadel surrendering on September 8. (By this time, at Wellington's urging, a new engineer corps had been formed and made a significant contribution to siege warfare from this period.)

At this stage of the war Wellington seemed unwilling to contemplate the invasion of France while part of Spain (Catalonia) was still occupied, but he was exhorted to advance to increase the pressure on France while Napoleon was totally committed in fighting against Britain's continental allies in the so-called War of Liberation in Germany. Writing to Bathurst on September 19, 1813, he stated that

I feel a great disinclination to enter the French territory under existing circumstances [including with] about 25,000 Spaniards, neither paid nor fed, and who must plunder, and will set the whole country against us . . . and matters on our right in Catalonia are not at all in the state in which they ought to be.

He conceded, however, that as the government had promised their allies that southern France would be invaded, "I think I ought, and will bend a little to the views of the Allies, if it can be done with safety to the army, notwithstanding that I acknowledge I should prefer to turn my attention to Catalonia."[23]

Wellington crossed the River Bidassoa, the important strategic barrier between Spain and France, on October 7, 1813, driving back the opposing French forces, and on October 31 Pamplona surrendered. Its governor, Gen. Louis-Pierre Cassan, had threatened to blow up the place before capitulating, entirely contrary to the contemporary "laws of war." To prevent this infringement of accepted conduct, Wellington had authorized Carlos de España, the Spanish general conducting the siege, to shoot Cassan, his officers and noncommissioned officers (NCOs), and one-tenth of his soldiers, had

Cassan carried out his threat. It seems a draconian measure but was acceptable under contemporary mores, and its threat was successful.

On November 1 Wellington issued a proclamation in French and Basque, addressed to the local inhabitants, stressing that he had ordered that no harm be done to civilians. He attached a translation of his General Order to his army on the need to respect private property and to treat the inhabitants with civility, as any misconduct toward the peaceable people of France "would be unmanly and unworthy of the nations to whom the Commander of the Forces now addresses himself." These strictures against plundering did not arise entirely from reasons of humanity. Throughout their occupation of Spain, the French had suffered grievously from Spanish guerrilla activity, which had not only inflicted countless casualties but had severely disrupted communications and tied up many thousands of troops who could have been deployed more usefully against the enemy field armies. Now that Wellington was operating in an enemy country, he sought to gain the trust of the locals and thus prevent any guerrilla operations against his forces, "similar and worse evils to the army at large than those which the enemy's army have suffered in the Peninsula."[24] This policy worked: far from being harassed by French partisans, Wellington's army received more cooperation from the French civilians than they accorded to their own army, which to them represented the authority which had imposed requisitions and conscription upon them for many years.

It meant, however, that Wellington was unable to permit many of his Spanish troops to enter France, their commissariat and government support being so inadequate that they would have had to plunder to subsist and thus alienate the local population. In November 1813 he wrote that his Spanish troops

> are in so miserable a state, that it is really hardly fair to expect that they will refrain from plundering a beautiful country, into which they enter as conquerors; particularly, adverting to the miseries which their own country has suffered from its invaders. . . .

In other words, it would have been understandable if the Spanish had plundered as a reprisal for years of ill treatment at the hands of the French in Spain. Wellington stated:

> If I could now bring forward 20,000 good Spaniards, paid and fed,
> I should have Bayonne. If I could bring forward 40,000, I do not
> know where I should stop . . . but I cannot venture to bring forward
> any for want of means of paying and supporting them. Without
> pay and food, they must plunder; and if they plunder, they will ruin
> us all.[25]

The conduct of the Spanish troops he did take into France realized
his fears. In the following month he wrote to their commander,
General Pablo Morillo, that

> I did not lose thousands of men to bring the army under my com-
> mand into the French territory, in order that the soldiers might plun-
> der and ill treat the French peasantry, in positive disobedience of
> my orders; and I beg that you and your officers will understand that
> I prefer to have a small army that will obey my orders, and preserve
> discipline, to a large one that is disobedient.[26]

From this period is recorded a glimpse of Wellington's style of
command that conflicts with the usual perception of his aloofness
and reserve. Harry Smith, a junior staff officer, recalled how
Wellington reconnoitered in the company of Sir George Murray
and three commanders from the Light Division. As he began to give
orders to Murray, the others made to leave, but Wellington said,
"Oh, lie still," and explained the reasons for his orders; Smith noted,
"It was one of the most interesting scenes I have ever witnessed."[27] It
is probably unlikely that this marks a change in Wellington's mode
of command, but it demonstrates clearly that he was prepared to
open up to those whose judgment he trusted (and the three officers
involved—Gens. Sir Charles Alten and James Kempt and Lt.-Col.
John Colborne—were among the most reliable in the army). Soult
continued to make a determined resistance; on November 10
Wellington attacked him at the Battle of Nivelle and forced the
French to withdraw in disorder, and on December 10 a French at-

tack was defeated at the Battle of the Nive. Another was repelled at St. Pierre on December 13, in which Rowland Hill gained the victory before Wellington arrived (he was said to have exclaimed, "Hill, the day is your own!"). This did, however, cause a measure of disquiet among some of Wellington's subordinates and raised a question. John Colborne stated, "Wellington committed a great error. Hill's Division was quite isolated," and yet after the victory Hill wrote an account of the affair, expecting it to be published, but "much to his disappointment," Wellington used it only to compile his own dispatch, in which little mention was made of Hill's part.[28]

Sir William Stewart, commander of the Second Division, was more upset than Hill, and Wellington was angered when he read in an English newspaper that Stewart and Hill had ordered their own reports to be circulated among their regiments. That anger (though directed at Stewart) is evident from Wellington's letters to Hill, which explained that "your dispatch did not come in till long after my report had been written; and it appeared to me that mine was so detailed as to render very little alteration necessary."[29] Furthermore, he claimed that he could not have sent in Hill's and Stewart's own dispatches without also submitting those of four other generals involved; and suspecting Stewart's motives for the reported circulation of his dispatch, Wellington was sufficiently incensed as to threaten to report Stewart to the Duke of York.

This could be regarded in the light of the need to report quickly and succinctly to the government in dispatches that did not have space to mention by name every unit or individual. Conversely, this episode could be interpreted as Wellington endeavoring to enhance his own reputation by reducing the significance of others, and it was not the only occasion on which individuals thought themselves insufficiently acknowledged. In December 1813, for example, William Napier complained, "I don't like Lord Wellington's despatch . . . the best thing done on the 10th November, 1813, was the attack of the 43rd Light Infantry, and he has not done us the honour to mention our names,"[30] although it appears from the remainder of this letter that Napier was not hugely offended. Perhaps most famously, Wellington's somewhat unfair treatment of the whole of the artillery in the Waterloo dispatch aroused considerable disquiet among members of that corps. Such views may only have reflected relatively private grievances, but their existence is significant as a contrast to the adulation emanating from other quarters and especially in subsequent years.

Wellington was certainly not unaware of his own importance and indeed seems to have turned it to his advantage. Much later, when speaking with admiration for Napoleon's military genius, he added,

> [N]o man has ever lost more armies than he did. Now with me the loss of every man told. I could not risk so much; I knew that if I ever lost five hundred men without the clearest necessity, I should be brought upon my knees to the bar of the House of Commons.[31]

Even if this were something of an exaggeration, increased fame brought its rewards: in mid-1813 he was reported as saying that having earned the confidence of the Allied powers, whatever he said or ordered was thought right even if it were wrong, so that he was able to do what others dare not attempt. The same applied to the troops:

> When I come myself, the soldiers think what they have to do the most important, since I am there, and that all will depend on their exertions . . . they will do for me what perhaps no one else can make them do.[32]

Driving on into France, Wellington's engineers threw a bridge over the River Adour, and on February 27 Soult was defeated at Orthez and the investment of Bayonne was completed. On March 12 Beresford and the Seventh Division entered Bordeaux, which like other places in the region had declared support for the Bourbon monarchy in preference to Napoleon, and on April 10 Wellington won his final battle of the Peninsular War at Toulouse. Soult evacuated the city on the following day. Tragically, this was an unnecessary action, for Napoleon had abdicated on April 6, ending the war. When the news reached Wellington on April 12, shortly after he had entered Toulouse, it provoked a rare display of emotion, as he spun on his heels and exclaimed, "Hurrah!"

More in character was the restrained language of his General Order of April 21:

> Upon congratulating the army upon this prospect of an honourable termination of their labors, the Commander of the Forces avails himself of the opportunity of returning the General Officers, Officers, and troops, his best thanks for their uniform discipline and gallantry in the field, and for their conciliating conduct towards the inhabitants of the country, which . . . have produced the fortunate circumstances that now hold forth to the world the prospect of genuine and permanent peace.[33]

The significance of the Peninsular War in the downfall of Napoleon's empire was considerable. In the widest context, the failure of Napoleon's own campaigns and his intransigence in not considering a negotiated settlement were crucial factors in his overthrow, but the attempt to fight a war on two fronts also contributed. The war in the Iberian Peninsula was a constant drain on his resources and its unpopularity damaged morale in the army. In considering the Peninsular War, Napoleon stated that

> that unlucky war ruined me; it divided my forces, obliged me to multiply my efforts, and caused my principles to be assailed. . . . All the circumstances of my disasters are connected with that fatal knot: it destroyed my moral power in Europe, rendered my embarrassments more complicated, and opened a school for the English soldiers . . . that unfortunate war in Spain was a real affliction, and the first cause of the calamities of France.[34]

Without the British support to Spain and Portugal, the French would surely never have been defeated, and in this regard Wellington's role in leading and animating his army was crucial. Despite the wishes contained in his General Order, however, both Wellington and his troops would be required to make one final exertion before the Napoleonic Wars were finally concluded.

The Hundred Days

By the conclusion of the Peninsular War, Wellington was established as his country's greatest soldier for some generations, and rewards were showered upon him. Most notably, on May 3, 1814, he was elevated to the highest rank of the peerage and became Duke of Wellington. When rewards had been proposed in the past, his family background had been the cause of some dissent: for example, when in May 1811 the Court of Common Council in London voted to present him with a sword worth 200 guineas, several members objected on the grounds that "the Wellesley family had been sufficiently paid," and similar feelings had been voiced by members of the parliamentary opposition.[1] The successful conclusion of the war, however, brought about something of a change. In May 1814 the government proposed a grant of £300,000 for Wellington to buy an estate, to which one of the government's leading critics, Samuel Whitbread, objected because it was too little. It was suggested that half a million pounds would not be too much, but after the Chancellor of the Exchequer reminded the members of Parliament that it was public money under consideration, a compromise was achieved and £400,000 was granted.

Despite the conclusion of hostilities, Wellington was not quite finished with the Peninsula; at the government's request he wrote a memorandum advising the newly restored King Ferdinand VII of Spain that he should moderate his conduct (which was ignored). On June 14, 1814, Wellington issued his final General Order on leaving his army, congratulating its members upon their part in "the recent events which have restored peace to their country and to the world," emphasizing his personal gratitude to them, and "he assures them that he shall never cease to feel the warmest interest in their welfare and honor; and that he will be at all times happy to be of any service to those whose conduct, discipline, and gallantry, their country is so much indebted."[2] Later in the month, in speeches to acknowledge his reception in both houses of Parliament, he repeated that "the gallantry and discipline of the troops" was a principal cause of his successes.[3]

Since the Wellesley brothers Richard and William had fallen out with Liverpool's ministry, it was not thought suitable for Wellington to take up a position in government, so instead he accepted the post of ambassador to France, "a situation for which I should never have thought myself qualified"; and he added, "I feel no objection to another absence in the public service, if it be necessary or desirable," even though he had been away from England for so many years.[4] There was, evidently, no very urgent desire to return to the domestic comforts of wife and family, although Kitty—now the duchess—joined him in June 1814. In Paris the duke was lionized by French high society, and evidently still susceptible to feminine charms, his name was linked with two of Napoleon's ex-mistresses, the opera singer Giuseppina Grassini and the actress Josephine Weimer, alias "Mademoiselle Georges."

In other respects, the appointment at Paris had its difficulties. The restored Bourbon monarchy was unpopular, support for the exiled Napoleon was growing, and the British cabinet came to have genuine fears about Wellington's personal safety. The duke was unenthusiastic about the suggestion that he should take command in North America, where the War of 1812 was continuing, so he was removed from Paris and appointed to replace Castlereagh (needed in

Parliament) as British plenipotentiary at the Congress of Vienna, where the Allied powers (and royalist France) were endeavoring to reshape the political dimensions of Europe after the Napoleonic era. This, like the Paris embassy, brought Wellington's diplomatic skills into sharp focus because he approached problems with a refreshing directness, as if conducting a military campaign. Even Talleyrand, the greatest French diplomat of his age, was impressed: he described how Wellington, instead of employing convoluted maneuvers as did many diplomats, used only prudence, watchfulness, and the experience of human nature. Talleyrand claimed that after months of nothing being accomplished, Wellington got the negotiations moving and that Wellington never found difficult that which others thought impractical. He appeared, said Talleyrand, to be an extraordinary statesman. Exaggerated as this may be, Wellington's approach does appear to have been rather more straightforward than that of Talleyrand himself or of the other great diplomatist of the period, Prince Klemens Metternich of Austria. (Talleyrand's remark on Wellington's use of previous experience was exemplified by the duke's comparison of Talleyrand, already mentioned, to one of Scindia's diplomats whom he had encountered in India).

The duke's diplomatic duties, however, were interrupted spectacularly: as an English stagecoach guard announced to some officers of the Twelfth Light Dragoons, "old Bonney has broken out again."[5] Not only had Napoleon escaped from the Mediterranean island of Elba, the territory that had been allowed him by the Allied powers, he had returned to France and been welcomed widely as a deliverer from the unpopular monarchy. The newly restored King Louis XVIII fled to the Netherlands and Napoleon regained his throne. The Allied powers, having suffered so long from the consequences of Napoleonic ambition, were in no mood to treat with him, and on March 13, 1815, the Congress declared him an outlaw and determined to remove him by force. Wellington was appointed to command the British troops already in the Netherlands, who were to be reinforced before the commencement of hostilities. The news of Wellington's appointment was greeted with rapture by the British troops. One wrote that he had never known such joy: "Nosey has got the command, won't we give them a drubbing now." They had no doubts about the outcome, he said, even if every member of the French army were a Napoleon.[6]

The army that Wellington was to lead, however, was not his old and experienced Peninsular force; some of his veteran units had been sent to America, while others had large numbers of recruits. His army now included a goodly proportion of troops from the newly constituted Kingdom of the Netherlands, including some who only the previous year had been marching under Napoleon's banner. Some others, such as the Hanoverians and Brunswickers, were also relatively inexperienced. On May 3 Wellington was appointed field marshal of the Netherlands, which at least gave him full authority over the troops of that nation, but relations with its sovereign, King William I, were strained. This led to the Duke's famous remark, "I have got an infamous army, very weak and ill equipped, and a very inexperienced staff," and this opinion was shared by many of the more experienced British observers.[7] One of the best-known comments was that by John Kincaid of the Ninety-Fifth, who did them little justice:

> We were, take all in all, a very bad army. Our foreign auxiliaries, who constituted more than half our numerical strength, with some exceptions, were little better than a raw militia—a body without a soul, or like an inflated pillow, that gives to the touch, and resumes its shape again when the pressure eases.[8]

Wellington's solution to the problem was in his organization of these forces. His formation of brigades and divisions blended the British and the others, the inexperienced with the veterans, in so effective a manner that the experienced bolstered the inexperienced so that with some exceptions the latter behaved with almost as much resolution as the battle-hardened.

Although a number of his old Peninsular colleagues were with him, Wellington complained about the absence of others and even suggested that those he wished to have were being withheld deliberately due to the patronage of the army establishment. Among those appointed with whom he had never before worked was the Earl of Uxbridge, and it was remarked that the latter's elopement with Wellington's sister-in-law would prevent them from cooperating effectively. Sir William Fraser recorded how the duke was told that "Lord Uxbridge has the reputation of running away with everybody he can," to which Wellington replied, "I'll take good care he don't run away with me: I don't care about anybody else" (though Fraser admitted, "I have been compelled to soften the vigorous vernacular of the Great Duke!").[9]

In another respect, the forthcoming campaign was unlike anything Wellington had experienced since his unfortunate cooperation with Cuesta in Spain: in 1815 he was not supreme commander but an equal partner in a coalition with the Prussian army of Field Marshal Gebhard Leberecht von Blücher. A seventy-three-year-old veteran who had served with great distinction, notably in the campaigns of 1813 and 1814, Blücher was a redoubtable fighter and a most passionate hater of Napoleon; he was ably assisted by his chief of staff, August Wilhelm von Gneisenau, a very capable officer but mistrustful of the British. Despite some subsequent British histories which (not unnaturally) concentrated on the British contribution, the successful outcome of the campaign was the result of collaboration, and indeed, without the presence of the Prussians, Wellington would surely never have been in a position to fight at Waterloo, much less to defeat Napoleon single-handedly.

The collaboration between Wellington and the Prussians raised questions, notably among the latter, from a fairly early date and has been highlighted by conflicting opinions among modern historians. Among accusations leveled against Wellington were that he behaved with duplicity toward the Prussians, both during the campaign and subsequently, by attempting to suppress critical comments to preserve his reputation. It is perhaps unlikely that these conflicting views of Wellington's conduct can be reconciled, but when considering the criticisms it is pertinent to consider his position. As commander of his own army, his responsibility was primarily toward the government of his own country and the preservation of his troops in the knowledge that a defeat, or being maneuvered away from his line of retreat and communications toward the Channel ports, could have had disastrous consequences. He was also a member of a coalition, with the other part on a level of parity with his own authority, unlike the later Peninsular War when his Spanish allies were under his own control. It was not impossible that this two-fold duty might lead to a conflict of interests, notwithstanding that his principal duty and desire was to defeat Napoleon.

Wellington once remarked, "I have acted according to the best of my judgment; and what the enemy says of me, and what they say of me at home, I do not care."[10] Similarly, his inclination was against the concept of published history. As early as May 1815 he commented,

> I have invariably refused to communicate to any person documents to enable him to write a history of the late war; as I consider the transactions too recent for any person to write a true history without hurting the feelings of nations, and of some individuals.[11]

This was to be his feeling throughout, but some concern for his reputation would have been only natural. Some hint of how he felt may be gleaned from the story of his sitting for Sir Thomas Lawrence in 1824 for a portrait destined for Sir Robert Peel. Lawrence portrayed him wearing his Waterloo cloak and holding a watch; Wellington demanded that a telescope replace the watch, lest the impression be given that at Waterloo he was waiting for Blücher to save the day, which, he averred, he was not, though actually it was the desperately awaited Prussian arrival that finally swung the course of the battle. Such anecdotes, perhaps, reveal the humanity behind the public face.

The two Allied armies in the Netherlands that were to confront Napoleon, Wellington's in the east and the Prussians in the west, remained separate. Napoleon's strategy was to use his practiced maneuver of striking rapidly at the junction of the enemy forces, massing against and overpowering one, then turning on the other. While it was known that Napoleon's forces were gathering, intelligence concerning their movements was difficult to obtain with certainty. As Wellington wrote on May 11,

> In the situation in which we are placed at present, neither at war nor at peace, unable on that account to patrole [*sic*] up to the enemy and ascertain his position by view . . . it is difficult, if not impossible, to combine an operation. All we can do is to put our troops in such a situation, as, in case of a sudden attack by the enemy, to render it easy to assemble.[12]

This gave Napoleon a decided advantage, and as late as June 13 Wellington believed that no attack was imminent and wrote "I think we are now too strong for him here."[13]

It was a severe miscalculation. Napoleon burst into action and attacked the Prussian forward positions on June 15, initiating the "Hundred Days" campaign (named from the length of time between Napoleon's return and his defeat). The system of communication between the frontier and the Allied headquarters and between Wellington in Brussels and the Prussians was not good, and there is considerable divergence of opinion as to when Wellington was apprised of the French offensive. The conventional British version is that news was only received in mid-afternoon on June 15; Prussian suspicions were that Wellington was informed rather earlier, was late responding, and then attempted to conceal his inaction. Indeed, the early British historian William Siborne changed his account between the first and third editions of his history to reflect the view of the earlier time of arrival. From late afternoon, however, orders were dispatched to put the army into motion, and in the evening Wellington attended one of the events of the Brussels social calendar, a ball given by the Duchess of Richmond. Wellington was said to have appeared anxious and distracted, as well he might, and it was at this event that he supposedly remarked, "Napoleon has humbugged me, by God." Doubts have been cast upon the veracity of this anecdote, but in effect it was true: Napoleon had gained the initiative, though in fairness to Wellington, he had to be certain of the direction of Napoleon's main advance before finalizing his own dispositions or risk being caught out even more severely than he was.

The forward posts of Wellington's army were at the crossroads of Quatre Bras, southeast of Brussels. Wellington had ordered a concentration west of that point, but the Netherlands troops in question had been posted at Quatre Bras by the capable and experienced Gen. Jean-Victor Constant Rebecque, chief of staff to the Prince of Orange, son of the King of the Netherlands and who was Wellington's deputy. This disobedience ultimately saved the day. Napoleon's main thrust was aimed at the Prussians at Ligny, to the east of Quatre Bras, and it was alleged that Wellington gave Blücher misleading information concerning his own positions and that the Prussians had only stood to fight on the understanding that they would receive help, though in fairness Wellington had offered support only if he were not attacked himself. As it happened, while Napoleon attacked the Prussians with his main body, his left wing under Marshal Michel Ney assailed the Allied troops at Quatre Bras. The Netherlands forces there hung on grimly until British reinforcements came up piecemeal later in the day, and the position was held, but the Prussians were forced back at Ligny, Blücher was unhorsed and temporarily put out of action, and Gneisenau had to conduct the beginning of their retreat. He was suspicious of Wellington but decided to fall back while remaining in touching distance of Wellington's army, thus frustrating Napoleon's scheme of driving the two Allied forces apart. When Blücher regained his headquarters, he insisted that all efforts be made to support Wellington. With the Prussians retiring, however, Wellington had to do likewise; on June 17, he headed north toward Brussels. He took up a position along a ridge by the village of Mont St. Jean, though his headquarters were situated a short distance to the north at Waterloo. The area was a good defensible position and had been reconnoitered a considerable time before, although it is possible that Wellington's preferred location was farther south on the ridge that was to be occupied by Napoleon, and had been altered by Wellington's chief of staff.

On the night of June 17, as the army lay without cover in weather as wet as anyone had experienced, another glimpse of Wellington's style of command may be detected. Uxbridge knew that he would have to take command on the morrow should Wellington be incapacitated but had no knowledge of the duke's plans and was afraid to ask. Finally, he dared. Wellington replied,

"Who will attack first tomorrow, I or Bonaparte?" "Bonaparte," said Uxbridge. "Well," continued the duke, "Bonaparte has not given me any idea of his projects: and as my plans depend on his, how can you expect me to tell you what mine are?" Then, giving Uxbridge a friendly pat on the shoulder, he said that one thing was certain: "Whatever happens, you and I will do our duty."[14] Although this may demonstrate Wellington's self-confidence, it was still potentially dangerous not even to discuss the general situation with a sound and experienced subordinate.

The course of the Battle of Waterloo is too familiar to be repeated here in detail. Napoleon switched the emphasis of his operations westward, leaving the smaller part of his army under Marshal Emmanuel Grouchy to pursue what he believed to be a defeated Prussian army while he attacked Wellington's position at Mont St. Jean. Heavy assaults were mounted against Wellington's line from the late morning of June 18, all of which were beaten back, Wellington's patchwork army holding firm thanks to the manner in which it had been deployed. The casualties were immense: John Kincaid, for example, remarked that he had never heard of a battle in which everyone was killed, but it seemed as if Waterloo would be such a one. Throughout the battle, Wellington seemed always to be at the most critical point, overseeing the fighting and even personally checking the unsteadiness of units that were being tested to a breaking point.

The style of Wellington's command in action had been observed during the Peninsular War. One officer described how

> he has nothing of the truncheon about him; nothing full-mouthed, important, or fussy: his orders, on the field, are all short, quick, clear and to the purpose. . . "you will give them a volley, and charge bayonets; but don't let your people follow them too far down the hill."[15]

The same was observed at Waterloo, and glimpses of him during the battle exemplify the reasons why he inspired the utmost confidence. Sir Augustus Frazer, commander of the horse artillery, remarked on

Wellington two days after the battle:

> Where, indeed, and what is not his forte? Cold and indifferent, nay, apparently careless in the beginning of battles, when the moment of difficulty comes intelligence flashes from the eyes of this wonderful man; he rises superior to all that can be imagined. . . . Several times were critical; but confidence in the duke, I have no doubt, animated every breast. His Grace exposed his person, not unnecessarily but nobly; without his personal exertions, his continual presence wherever and whenever more than usual exertions were required, the day had been lost.[16]

A junior staff officer, James Shaw, recalled an example when he reported to Wellington that a gap had opened in the line.

> This very startling information he received with a degree of coolness, and replied to in an instant with such precision and energy, as to prove the most complete self-possession; and left on my mind the impressions that his Grace's mind remained perfectly calm during every phase, however serious, of the action; that he felt confident of his own powers of being able to guide the storm which raged around him; and from the determined manner in which he then spoke, it was evident that he had resolved to defend to the last extremity every inch of the position which he then held.

Ordering Shaw to bring up all the troops and artillery he could find, Wellington then personally led the Brunswick corps to plug the gap:

> In no other part of the action was the Duke of Wellington exposed to so much personal risk as on this occasion . . . at no other period of the day were his great qualities as a commander so strongly brought out, for it was the moment of his greatest peril as to the result of the action.[17]

As the afternoon wore on, salvation appeared on Wellington's left flank in the form of Blücher's Prussians. Leaving one corps at

Wavre to hold back Grouchy, Blücher had marched the remainder of his army in the promised support of Wellington, compelling Napoleon to commit part of his army to keeping back the Prussians on his right flank. David Robertson of the Ninety-second Highlanders recalled with every justification that when the Prussians appeared, "Never was reprieve more welcome to a death-doomed criminal."[18]

Napoleon's final, desperate attempt to break Wellington's line was an attack by the infantry of the Imperial Guard—the Middle rather than the Old Guard as sometimes stated—and again Wellington was on hand to direct its repulse. As the head of the French columns approached the crest of Wellington's ridge, he ordered the British Foot Guards, who had been lying down under cover, to rise up. Several versions of his exact words are recorded; they were probably (to the general in command), "Now, Maitland, now's your time," followed by something like "Stand up, Guards!" Their disciplined musketry was seconded by a flank attack on one French column executed by Sir John Colborne's Fifty-second Light Infantry; as the French attack recoiled, Wellington urged Colborne to "go *on*, go *on*!" The duke raised his hat as a signal for a general advance, and as he rode along the line called out to the exultant troops, "No cheering, my lads, but forward, and complete your victory."[19]

Near the end of the battle Uxbridge, riding alongside Wellington, provoked one of the most famous Wellingtonian anecdotes when a grapeshot hit his leg. Uxbridge reputedly looked down and said, "By God, sir, I've lost my leg," to which Wellington is supposed to have replied, "By God, sir, so you have!" It was little short of astonishing that Wellington should have remained unscathed throughout the battle while his staff fell around him: two of his ADCs were killed, his chief of staff mortally wounded (Sir William DeLancey, Deputy Quartermaster-General), and his military secretary, Fitzroy Somerset, lost an arm. Indeed, toward the end of the battle, when it was obvious that Napoleon had been defeated, one of his remaining aides rebuked the duke for riding too near to the retreating enemy, saying that his life was too valuable to be thrown away. Wellington made the fairly startling reply that as the battle was won, his life was of no consequence, so let them fire away. Well might he have remarked that the finger of Providence had been upon him and, even more forcibly as he ate supper that night, "The hand of Almighty God has been upon me this day."[20]

Wellington met Blücher near the aptly named inn of La Belle Alliance in what had been the rear of Napoleon's position in the late evening. The Prussians agreed to continue pursuing Napoleon's disintegrating army; Wellington's forces were simply too exhausted. The duke rode back to his headquarters at Waterloo, where he gave up his bed to his favorite aide, the wounded Sir Alexander Gordon, while he took a brief sleep upon a pallet. His surgeon, Dr. John Hume, awoke him with news of Gordon's death and with a list of casualties. Wellington wept openly and said that he thanked God he didn't know what it was like to lose a battle but that nothing could be more painful than to win one with the loss of so many friends. After a cup of tea and some toast he wrote his official dispatch, a succinct account well-composed for one who must have still been in a state of emotional shock, though not without its flaws (some thought themselves ill-rewarded for not being mentioned). In his usual restrained style Wellington reported that "the army never, upon any occasion, conducted itself better," and in a brief note to his brother William said it was the most desperate battle he had ever fought and that he was never so near being beaten.[21] To his old colleague Beresford he wrote,

> Never did I see such a pounding match. Both were what the boxers called gluttons. Napoleon did not manoeuvre at all. He just moved forward in the old style, in columns, and was beaten off in the old style. . . . I never saw the British infantry behave so well.[22]

It had been, he told Thomas Creevey, "the nearest run thing you ever saw," and that he didn't think it would have turned out as it did had he not been there. That was surely the unvarnished truth.

The Statesman

ON THE evening of Waterloo, Wellington remarked, "I have never fought such a battle, and I trust I shall never fight another one."[1] This hope, expressed more than once, was to be fulfilled: his battlefield career ended on the evening of June 18, 1815. For that he can have had no regrets; he seems to have been seriously affected by the carnage in which he had played so crucial a role. When visiting the mortally wounded Sir William DeLancey immediately after Waterloo, he said that he never wished to see another battle: "It has been too much to see such brave men, so equally matched, cutting each other to pieces."[2] Later he told his friend Lady Shelley that although he was always too preoccupied to feel any emotion while in action, he later experienced what might now be recognized as a form of depression, of exhaustion in mind and spirit; and he said that next to a battle lost, the greatest misery was a battle won.

Waterloo did not bring about an immediate cessation of hostilities, but after it Napoleon had no hope. He abdicated again and the Allied powers exiled him to St. Helena while the Bourbon monarchy was restored to the throne of France for a second time. As the victor of Waterloo and Napoleon's final destroyer, Wellington was elevated to the status of peerless hero. The Prussians' contribution was not overlooked, but in British popular perception their crucial role did not, perhaps, assume the importance it merited. The remaining thirty-seven years of the duke's life were to see him transformed from successful general to national icon, but not without troubles along the way.

Wellington was appointed commander in chief of the Allied army of occupation of France on October 22, 1815; the presence of Allied troops in that country was to last until November 1818. Harry Smith, a staff officer during the occupation, recalled how Wellington was scrupulously fair in addressing any complaints about the occupying forces' behavior in their dealings with French civilians. The duke, he claimed, stated that his troops should pride themselves on their deportment and that that pride should not be injured in his keeping.

Wellington received a noted tribute from a grateful nation in the purchase of an estate, with a handsome house, Stratfield Saye in Hampshire, for some £263,000, considerably less than the amount granted by Parliament. The architect Benjamin Wyatt proposed building a grand new mansion akin to that constructed for another general who had defeated a previous generation of French armies, the Duke of Marlborough's Blenheim Palace, but Wellington was content with the existing property. He did, however, make some improvements to the London residence that he acquired in 1817, Apsley House (known as "Number One, London"). These fine properties were not the home he would have liked; his wife, the duchess, was not suited to the life of a society hostess. She was not an especially competent manager of household accounts, which caused the duke much frustration, and they grew further apart. Despite his proverbially reserved nature, to close friends he confided his unhappiness, claiming that the duchess was unable to provide either domestic comfort or intellectual stimulation. It was reported that when a lady asked him whether he had "inspired a great deal of admiration, and enthusiasm among women," he replied, "Oh, yes, plenty of that! plenty of that! but no woman ever loved me: never in my whole life."[3] If that conversation were reported correctly, it is perhaps a sad reflection on his perception of his wife's undoubted and genuine affection.

Without a solid domestic foundation, the society the duke was anxious to enjoy was supplied less by family than by a circle of close friends, including Sarah, Countess of Jersey, and Harriet, wife of his devoted friend Charles Arbuthnot. Invariably there were suggestions of impropriety, as before, in these cases apparently unsubstantiated. In 1815–16 his friendship with Lady Frances Wedderburn-Webster had been questioned (the duke had been sufficiently concerned for her safety to spare time, on the morning of the Battle of Waterloo, to write a note advising her to prepare to leave Brussels for Antwerp in case he had to leave the city unprotected), and there were even suggestions that her husband might file for divorce on the grounds that a "criminal conversation" had occurred. The Websters eventually sued a newspaper proprietor who had published the gossip.

Perhaps the most celebrated case concerning the duke and a reported liaison was that involving the courtesan Harriette Wilson, who at one time had plied her trade from the London establishment of the notorious Mrs. Porter, which Wellington does seem to have frequented prior to his marriage. In 1824 Harriette Wilson wrote her memoirs, and her publisher, Joseph Stockdale, attempted to blackmail the duke with threats to include him in the story unless he paid for the relevant passages to be removed. Whatever Wellington actually replied, the meaning was conveyed in the legendary blast, "Publish and be damned." The memoirs appeared in 1825 with the Wellington stories included; the duke did not deny knowing her, but the revelations—probably greatly embroidered—do not seem to have damaged his reputation. If Wellington lacked a satisfactory home life, he had a great deal of public duty to occupy his time. Indeed, such were the calls upon him for most of the rest of his life that on one occasion, at age seventy, he claimed,

> Every other animal—even a donkey—a costermonger's donkey—is allowed some rest, but the Duke of Wellington never! There is no

help for it. As long as I am able to go on, they will put the saddle upon my back and make me go on.[4]

The appointments he took up were in some cases, not unnaturally, connected with military affairs, but he also entered political life again, though not as an inflexible "party" man. While adhering to the principles of the Tory party that was still in office, he made it clear that his duty was to the country before the party and that he would not become part of an obstructive opposition should the fortunes of the ministry be reversed. Nevertheless, he had little sympathy for the opposition Whigs and Radicals who would, he believed, cause the ruination of the country should they be installed as a government. His background and instincts tended toward the perception that democracy equated with mob rule and the chaos of the French Revolution and that the natural state of government was that those in the higher echelons of society should rule, a perception not uncommon at the time.

Wellington's first appointment, in December 1818, was as Master General of the Ordnance, responsible for the army's ordnance services, including artillery and engineers, and because it gave him a seat in the cabinet he could also act as the ministry's military adviser. This included the control of civil unrest, of which there was a considerable amount in the years following the end of the Napoleonic Wars, the product principally of economic hardships. By instinct and inclination, Wellington feared the specter of revolution and thus evinced little sympathy for those who disturbed the peace for any reason. When, for example, there was unrest in the agricultural areas of southern and eastern England in 1830, including the burning of barns and ricks and the destruction of agricultural machinery, he urged the magistrates of Hampshire to organize armed and mounted units of their outdoor servants to attack and arrest any mob. He claimed that the local gentry's activity was the best way of quieting the unrest, rather than involving the military in this unpleasant duty.

Wellington's fear and hatred of mob rule can only have been heightened by incidents in which his previous status as the country's military idol seemed to be replaced by widespread unpopularity. This was first evident in 1820 during the friction between King George IV and his errant queen, Caroline of Brunswick. The queen received much popular support, but Wellington, though thoroughly disapproving of the king's wayward lifestyle, believed it his duty to support his sovereign, and as a consequence attracted the earnest disapproval of those who took Caroline's side. The duke was hooted and hissed at in the street and on one occasion was actually attacked.

In his personal life as well, the early 1820s was not his best period. He must have experienced much anguish at the deteriorating relationship with the duchess, and although he was generally happy to entertain children, his own sons do not seem to have received much affection from him. Ill health also exerted a toll: to treat an eardrum damaged by a gun that discharged while the duke inspected at Woolwich, a distinguished aural specialist injected a caustic solution that destroyed his hearing on the left side and caused him protracted agony.

A heavy blow at this time concerned Wellington's old political ally, Lord Castlereagh, at that time himself suffering great unpopularity: his support for the political emancipation of Roman Catholics alienated many of those who agreed with him over his opposition to other political reforms. In 1822 Castlereagh showed evidence of mental instability, and as his friend Wellington told him, "'From what you have said, I am bound to warn you that you cannot be in your right mind.' He was sitting or lying on a sofa, and said, 'Since you say so I fear it must be so.'"[5] Only days later Castlereagh killed himself by cutting his throat. It was thought that Wellington might take over as foreign secretary, but he had no inclination for the post. The position went to George Canning, a politician Wellington disliked, but he still recommended him to the king as being the best man available.

The death of the Duke of York in January 1827 caused the post of commander in chief to become vacant. Wellington was appointed as the obvious choice, but his tenure at this point was not to be of long duration. The prime minister, Lord Liverpool, suffered a paralytic stroke and had to leave office, and Canning was appointed as his successor. After having received what he considered to be an insulting letter from Canning, Wellington resigned both as Master General of the Ordnance (which, as it was a cabinet post, was explicable for political reasons) and as commander in chief, a resignation only explicable on the grounds of his dislike of Canning. Almost the whole front bench resigned with him, Canning's accession having split the Tory party, but his ministry was not destined to last very long. Canning caught a cold at the funeral of the Duke of York and never fully recovered; he died in August 1827 and Wellington was reinstalled as commander in chief under Canning's successor as prime minister, Lord Goderich. His ineffectual regime ended early in the following year, and though not enthusiastic about taking on the job, Wellington acceded to the king's request to form the next administration.

On January 9, 1828, Wellington took up the post of prime minister. His tenure in office was beset with a number of substantial difficulties. He found his preferred style of command at odds with conventional politics, with cabinet colleagues not prepared to accept military-style commands:

> [T]hey agree to what I say in the morning, and then in the evening they start up with some crochet which deranges the whole plan. . . . I have been accustomed to carry on things in quite a different manner; I assembled my officers and laid down my plan, and it was carried into effect without any more words.[6]

His cabinet lacked harmony: William Huskisson, the colonial secretary, ended their somewhat uneasy association by resigning over the eradication of two "rotten boroughs" (parliamentary seats lacking a fair electoral system), and the other leading Canningites went with him. Wellington brought into his cabinet men more to his liking, including Sir George Murray, his old chief of staff from the Peninsula days, and Sir Henry Hardinge, another friend who had been the duke's liaison officer with the Prussian army in 1815. The question of Catholic emancipation, however, was a much more difficult problem.

Attempts to relieve Roman Catholics of the political strictures had bedeviled more than one administration. William Pitt had resigned in 1801 over royal intransigence on the matter; King George III believed that such a measure would be contrary to his coronation oath. Wellington himself came from the Protestant landed class in Ireland and indeed was regarded by some as representative of it: for example, in 1814 it was reported that a sign on a newly erected row of buildings in Ireland, "Wellington Place," was torn down at the instigation of the local priest, who declared the duke to be an enemy of the Roman Catholic religion. Despite his background, however, Wellington's fear of insurrection and that that country might become ungovernable led him to deduce that emancipation was the only practical course. He stated that to have maintained a solidly anti-Catholic ministry would have cost him ministers and support and "what I looked to as the great advantage of the measure was that it would unite all men of property and character together in one interest against the agitators."[7]

This display of pragmatism, for all its necessity, proved to be one of the hardest fights of Wellington's career; indeed, he compared it to a field of battle that had to be fought out. He eventually won over the king with much persuasion of the measure's absolute necessity, and finally with a threat of resignation, but the most intractable of the duke's opponents could not be dealt with by logical argument. For his support of Catholic emancipation, Wellington attracted considerable opprobrium in the popular media. Cartoons, for example, portrayed him and his colleague Sir Robert Peel as the murderers Burke and Hare—the notorious Edinburgh criminals brought to justice in 1829 for the killing of numerous victims whose bodies they sold for medical research—smothering the constitution in the interest of promoting Catholicism, while another depicted Wellington as a lobster (a nickname for a soldier, derived from the traditional British red coat) wearing a monk's habit and festooned with rosary beads. The most insulting was a letter published in *The Standard* newspaper. The Earl of Winchilsea, one of the most vociferous opponents of emancipation, accused Wellington of dishonesty in using the proposed measure as a step toward implementing "his insidious designs for the infringement of our liberties, and the introduction of Popery in every department of the State." Winchilsea declined to apologize, and Wellington challenged him to a duel. On the morning of March 21, 1829, the two met at Battersea to settle this point of honor. Wellington told his second, the faithful Hardinge, not to place Winchilsea so near a ditch, for "if I hit him he will tumble in."[8] Wellington deliberately fired wide, Winchilsea in the air; the latter then made a grudging apology and the duke bid him good morning, later in the day reporting to the king that he had just fought a duel. It was the last time that a British prime minister settled an argument by such drastic means.

The Bill for Catholic Relief was passed by Parliament on April 10, and the Emancipation Act received royal assent on April 13. It was the most significant achievement of Wellington's ministry, but not the only one: also of special note was the establishment of the Metropolitan Police, and while Peel is most closely associated with this foundation of a modern police service, Wellington had advocated it years earlier. Nevertheless, his administration only limped on, with opposing factions making party unity impossible. The death of King George IV in June 1829 (his brother succeeded him as King William IV) brought about a general election, in which the Tories were returned, though Wellington was evidently tiring of his position and offered to stand aside so that his friend Peel might become prime minister. He stayed on, though, as the political situation deteriorated, having lost much support from the more traditional Tories over the Emancipation Act. The situation worsened after Huskisson's death—he was hit by George Stephenson's locomotive "Rocket" at the opening of the Liverpool-Manchester railroad in September 1830 as the duke watched in horror.

Agitation for parliamentary reform, to which Wellington was resolutely opposed (as he declared to considerable shock in the House of Lords), was now reaching a crescendo. The prospect of a greater degree of democracy in the choosing of parliamentary representatives was contrary to all his political and personal philosophy, but he also had practical reasons for resisting reform, believing that strong government could not be delivered without the patronage exercised by the "owners" of rotten boroughs. The tide for reform, however, was unstoppable: the government's support crumbled, and it was defeated on November 15, 1830, on a vote on a minor concern, an amendment to the Civil List. Wellington realized that his position was untenable and resigned on the following day, though he later expressed his regrets about the decision.

Earl Grey formed a ministry and was intent on reform; Wellington spoke against the Reform Bill in the House of Lords, claiming that it would destroy the constitution. Grey, however, was faced with defeat over the bill, so he urged the king to dissolve Parliament, which he did on April 22, 1831. At that moment, however, Wellington had more personal concerns than matters of state: he was at the bedside of his wife, who died on April 24 after an illness of some length. Theirs had never been a felicitous union, Kitty's devotion to Wellington not being matched by her ability to provide him with the home life he desired, but he was genuinely much saddened by her death. Perhaps, as he reflected himself, he had only come to appreciate her fully at the moment he lost her. And at that moment, and not for the only time during the reform agitation, a mob smashed the windows in Apsley House.

Reform supporters triumphed in the general election, but the second attempt to pass a Reform Bill was defeated in the House of Lords; there was widespread rioting—especially severe in Bristol—and Wellington's windows were again broken. Faced with such opposition, Grey resigned and in May 1832 Wellington was asked to form a new ministry. After a few days of trying it became obvious that he could not find enough Tories to support his position of only moderate reform, and he abandoned the attempt. Grey returned to office, the opponents of the bill bowed to the inevitable, and the Reform Act passed into law on June 7, 1832. Its main effect was to give greater representation to the growing urban, industrialized towns, but Wellington remained firm in his opposition, fearing the threat of revolution such as what had recently unseated King Charles X of France. His opinion of the "reformed" Parliament was a laconic "I never saw so many shocking bad hats in my life."[9]

Wellington's opposition to reform led to an even greater degree of unpopularity: in June 1832 he was seriously threatened by a mob in London and had to be protected by two Chelsea pensioners; stones were thrown and there was a danger that he might be dragged from his horse. It was seventeen years to the day since his victory at Waterloo, and the public reaction could hardly have been more different.

From this period, however, Wellington's rehabilitation with the public began. He continued to speak in Parliament—as the great parliamentarian, prime minister, and orator William Ewart Gladstone remarked, always with a valid point and never for the sake of it— and remained in public life. As Lord Warden of the Cinque Ports he had the use of Walmer Castle, which he loved, and in 1843 he became Chancellor of Oxford University. Nor was he quite done with political life. In 1834 the government fell, and William IV asked the duke to form a new one. Wellington advised the king to appoint Peel instead, but as he was abroad the duke undertook to keep the government going, acting as prime minister and heading not only the Treasury but the ministries of home, foreign and colonial affairs, and war. This unprecedented concentration of authority, exercised without abuse, lasted for some three weeks, from mid-November until the second week of December, until Peel returned and constructed his own cabinet, unhampered by any previous appointments (which had been Wellington's reason for not making any temporary arrangements beyond a provisional appointment of Lord Chancellor). Wellington remained as foreign secretary until the following April, when upon Peel's resignation he left political office for the last time.

From this period Wellington took on some aspects of the archetypal elder statesman and clearly entranced the young Queen Victoria, who succeeded her uncle as sovereign in 1837. Despite advancing years, the duke remained very active, and it was from this time that he made his remark, mentioned above, about how he was more over-worked than a costermonger's donkey. That he was willing to continue to act in an advisory capacity can only be attributed to an unfailing sense of duty, though he claimed he had never tried to impose advice without being asked. On leaving active command of the army, he said he had determined never to interfere in any appointment or give advice unless requested, "and I never have. I have very often stated my views and given my advice—but never unless I was applied to."[10]

In 1842, however, he took on more than an advisory position when he succeeded his old companion Lord Hill as commander in chief. His tenure in this position in the last decade of his life is sometimes characterized as the laying of a dead hand upon the development of the army, but this can be overstated. During this period there was considerable tactical and technological development and reform, even though all Wellington's experience led him to rely on the characteristics of the past. It is hardly surprising that the duke remembered the organization that had served him so well in his campaigns. Sir George Browne recalled how he once reported finding the Ninety-seventh Foot in an excellent state of training, with "no newfangled notions, either in their dress or appointments," to which the duke replied, "I am very glad to hear it, very glad indeed. Depend upon it, there is nothing like them in the world in the shape of infantry."[11] Although not in the forefront of military reform—in fact rather the reverse—Wellington did, for example, sanction the first universal issue of a rifled musket, the Minié, to the British army in 1851. His opinions on this subject demonstrate his reliance on experience: he was less concerned with the enhanced accuracy of the new weapon than with ease of loading, suggesting a preference for volume of musketry, which had been the most important factor in his own campaigns, rather than accuracy. He insisted that the existing bore be retained to avoid any difficulties in the field had old and smaller-bored new weapons been in use concurrently, given the delay that would inevitably arise until the Minié could be issued universally. He also favored the heavier traditional bullet for its enhanced striking-power, and a further practical consideration for retaining the existing bore was that it would have been possible to use up existing stocks of ammunition had the Minié cartridges run out. The duke did, however, insist on the term "rifled musket" rather than "rifle," for remembering the small force of elite riflemen who had served under his command, he explained, "we must not allow them to fancy they are all riflemen, or they will become conceited, and be wanting next to be dressed in green, or some other jack-a-dandy uniform."[12]

Wellington's sense of duty again came to the fore in 1846 over the repeal of the Corn Laws. He stated that he had attempted to manage the House of Lords in support of the government on important matters and to use his influence to prevent a difference between the two chambers, which could have had a disruptive effect on the governance of the country. "I am the servant of the Crown and People. I have been paid and rewarded, and I consider myself retained, and that I can't do otherwise than serve as required when I can do so without dishonour"; it was a personal belief seemingly unchanged from his declaration some four decades earlier that he had eaten the king's salt, as was said in India, and was thus bound to service. To Lord Stanley, later Earl of Derby, he wrote, "You should advise the House to vote that which would lead most to publick [sic] order and would be most beneficial to the immediate interests of the country," and that he would always cooperate in whatever promoted order and good government.[13] Consequently, he made a most influential speech in the House of Lords that led to the passing of the repeal of the Corn Laws. The decisive vote took place in the early hours of the morning, and when Wellington left the House of Lords he found a crowd of workmen awaiting the glad news. They cheered him and cried, "God bless you, Duke!" "For Heaven's sake, people, let me get on my horse!" was his reply: it was just what might have been expected three decades and more before, to a regiment cheering "Our Arthur."

Peel's ministry did not long survive the repeal of the Corn Laws, a measure that had aroused wide opposition within his own party. A coalition of opposition and dissatisfied members of his own party defeated him on an Irish Coercion Bill the same day that the Lords passed the Corn Law repeal. Peel resigned four days later. The leader of the succeeding Whig ministry, Lord John Russell, approached Wellington with a view to obtaining the support of some of the Peelites, but the duke declined, claiming that coalitions were neither creditable to the individuals involved nor trusted by the public. As commander in chief, however, he pledged his personal support to the new administration and made it clear that when members of his own party sought his advice, he would never act against the sitting government, continuing to follow the higher ideal of duty rather than the constraints of party politics.

By this period Wellington had transcended any unpopularity and had become almost a living monument to a previous age, a representative of past glories, and still a fount of advice. His continuing role as commander in chief also helped to keep him in the forefront of public life, for example, in making unobtrusive military preparations to counter possible civil disturbance in London at the time of the Chartist unrest in 1848, fortunately unnecessary. The advancing years, however, deprived Wellington of his dearest friends: his confidant Harriet Arbuthnot had died in 1834, and her husband Charles, who had remained one of his closest friends, died in August 1850, only weeks after Sir Robert Peel was fatally injured in a fall from his horse. He and Wellington had not always been on the best of terms, though had been one of the duke's closest political colleagues.

Wellington's lifestyle remained largely unchanged. Never extravagant, his personal habits were still almost frugal, as exemplified by his bedroom at Walmer, a characteristically unostentatious chamber in which he slept upon a plain camp bed, as he had used on campaign. He seems, however, to have been an excellent host and remained close to many of his old military companions, who gathered annually for the Waterloo banquet, the most notable assembly of military distinction imaginable. The duke still enjoyed the company of the young, and anecdotes describe his great kindness toward children, although he was never especially close to his own sons. Despite the advancing years he continued to ride or walk to his office at Horse Guards, the center of army administration, except in bad weather, and always alone. All those he passed, it was said, greeted him, and all were acknowledged by a salute with two fingers of his right hand touching the brim of his hat.

Wellington's reaction to public adulation was unchanging, and in old age this was joined by a dislike of being helped. First, he did not want to emphasize the effects of advancing years, and second, he believed that those offering assistance did so just to say that they had. On one occasion he was hesitating crossing the busy road to Apsley House when a man almost as old as himself held up the traffic. Upon reaching the other curb the duke thanked him, whereupon the man removed his hat and declared that in a long life, "never did I hope to reach the day when I might be of the slightest assistance to the greatest man who ever lived." "Don't be a damned fool!" was Wellington's answer.[14]

Wellington never seems to have been in doubt about his own status or importance, and while steadfastly refusing to make any public comment on his actions, he was conscious enough of his reputation for posterity to permit his dispatches to be published (albeit with names omitted in statements that might reflect badly on those involved). Lord Brougham commented to John Gurwood, who edited the dispatches, "You have published a book that will live when we are in the dust and forgotten," to which the duke said, "Very true, so it will," when he heard the compliment.[15] Gurwood, an officer who had served under the duke, took his own life in 1845, pressure of work on the project being one of the causes ascribed at the time. Demonstrating one of the more unfortunate aspects of his character, Wellington wrote to the widowed Mrs. Gurwood, claiming that her husband had been in the habit of recording the duke's conversations, which clearly he thought a quite heinous act (overlooking, perhaps, the value of James Boswell's account of Samuel Johnson's sayings), and demanding the surrender of her late husband's papers, apparently not believing the lady's assurance that all relevant material had been burned. This pursuit at a time of mourning was hardly edifying, and presumably he was unaware of Lord Mahon's (later Earl of Stanhope) assiduous recording of his conversations at the same time. *The Dispatches*—of which a supplementary series was published by the second duke from 1852— reveal Wellington's great grasp of his business, and it would not be surprising if in later years he had some concern for his reputation. In 1842, for example, he produced a memorandum on the Waterloo campaign for Sir Francis Egerton (later Earl of Ellesmere) to use in refuting the account of the historian Sir Archibald Alison; by which, the duke said, according to the story told by Charles Arbuthnot, they would "make out Alison to be a d——d rascally Frenchman."[16]

Although Wellington could hardly be accused of self-effacement and of not recognizing his own importance, this was not manifested by undue bombast. In 1836 Lady Salisbury, one of his closer friends, asked whether his victory at Waterloo made him realize immediately "how infinitely you had raised your name above every other." Wellington replied that that would be vanity, whereas his first thought was for the public service; yet he agreed that he did experience a feeling of superiority, but only in his own trade:

> Perhaps there is no man now existing who would like to meet me on a field of battle; in that line I am superior. But when the war is over and the troops disbanded, what is your great general more than anybody else? . . . I am necessarily inferior to every man in his own line, though I may excel him in others. I cannot saw and plane like a carpenter, or make shoes like a shoemaker, or understand cultivation like a farmer. Each of these, on his own ground, meets me on terms of superiority. I feel I am but a man.[17]

It was probably the belief in his superiority in his own line as much as his background that led to the criticisms leveled against him, all perhaps with a degree of validity. He was accused of egotism, of being dictatorial, reactionary, and at least superficially, cold and unyielding. The latter is exemplified by the epithet "the Iron Duke," which was current in his lifetime (mentioned in 1845 by *Punch* magazine in relation to his unpolished style of writing), though Edward Pakenham had described him as an "iron man" and Wellington himself had referred to using a "hand of iron" to exert discipline in his army. Although the term may not have been common during the duke's life, it was sufficiently familiar to be used as the name of the 1870 battleship HMS *Iron Duke* and for another of 1912 that appropriately served as the flagship of Sir John Jellicoe at the Battle of Jutland in 1916. Among the criticisms, the Duke of York evidently thought Wellington unwilling to praise others lest it detracted from his own achievements (and the duke himself admitted that he should have been more fulsome in his acknowledgment of the efforts of others), but conversely the confidence in his own ability and apparent lack of self-doubt must have been a considerable contributory factor toward his successes.

During these last years of Wellington's life, he was known universally as just "the Duke," as if no other holder of such a peerage existed. Even iron dukes, however, could not go on indefinitely. Despite the restrictions of old age, Wellington remained the faithful elder statesman whose advice was always sought, notably by Queen Victoria, who relied on his wise counsel. In the closing stages of his life the specter of a new conflict with France appeared on the horizon when Prince Louis Napoleon, nephew of the great Napoleon whom Wellington had helped to defeat, was elected president of France in December 1848 and increased his power to the extent that he would become emperor in 1852. It was, perhaps, fitting that Wellington's last speech in the House of Lords concerned a military measure not unrelated to the perceived threat from France: the reconstitution of the militia that had largely fallen into neglect after the Napoleonic Wars. The reform of this "constitutional force," as he called it, was to provide successive generations with a valuable support, as he predicted it would.

Active to the end, Wellington arrived at Walmer Castle for his autumn sojourn on August 25, 1852, where he entertained a diplomatic guest, the Grand Duke of Mecklenburg-Strelitz and his duchess. After their departure he settled into his normal routine, and it was at this time that he made his famous remark—to his old friend John Wilson Croker and his wife—that the whole business of life, as in war, was endeavoring to find out what was not known from what was known, which he called "guessing what was on the other side of the hill." The old duke was fast approaching the other side of his own hill. He dined as usual on September 13, but on the following morning his servants found him ill. An apothecary and doctor were summoned, and after what appeared to be some fits they conveyed him to his armchair in his frugally furnished bedroom. With his younger son and daughter-in-law beside him, he slipped away in mid-afternoon, never regaining consciousness, so quietly that his passing could scarcely be discerned.

From the outpouring of sorrow at Wellington's death, it might have seemed that Britannia herself had been widowed. Queen Victoria was devastated with grief and ordered that the funeral be delayed until Parliament would convene in November, when a full state funeral, such as that accorded to another commoner, Horatio Nelson, would take place and that the duke would be laid to rest in St. Paul's Cathedral. Wellington's coffin lay in state at the Royal Military Hospital at Chelsea, where an endless stream of people filed past to pay their respects. The first to arrive, the queen, was so overcome that she had to be led away in tears. The funeral that followed on November 18 was an immense affair, such as hardly ever witnessed before or since, with military detachments, hundreds of thousands of spectators, and a funeral carriage of gigantic proportions weighing eighteen tons, ornamented with military trophies, and, to the eyes of many, unbearably ugly. Sir William Fraser, who was part of the Guard of Honor at the duke's lying in state and whose father had fought under Wellington in the Peninsula and at Waterloo, remarked: "There seemed to be a want of Simplicity; and in its place an amount of geegaw which was not in character with either the circumstances, or the man."[18]

As might have been expected, the national tributes to Wellington were fulsome. Perhaps they were influenced by the fact that Wellington's death also represented the passing of an age in a society that was changing rapidly. He was a product of the mid-eighteenth century, with all that that entailed, but had survived into the world of the Industrial Revolution, a world that could hardly have been conceived at the time of his birth. The last British officer to serve at Waterloo lived until 1891, the last "other rank" until 1892, but Wellington's death must have represented the passing of the generation that had fought one of the longest and most expensive wars in which the country had ever engaged, a war that had established Britain firmly on the European stage. The death of the duke must at the time have seemed all the more poignant for that, as if one of the supports of the nation itself had been removed.

Typical of the coverage of the funeral was that accorded by *The Illustrated London News,* which recorded: "The grave has closed over the mortal remains of the greatest man of our age, and one of the purest-minded men recorded in history." It also compared him, as have historians subsequently, with Napoleon:

> What a contrast is offered by [Wellington's] history to that of the mighty rival whom he so happily overthrew. Napoleon Bonaparte was false to liberty, a traitor and breaker of his word, a selfish despot. . . . But to every principle to which Bonaparte was false, Wellington was true. The British hero was utterly unselfish, his word was truth itself, his guiding star was public duty, his cause was that of freedom and humanity, and his successes were as brilliant and beneficial as the final defeat of his great antagonist was signal and calamitous. Wellington never fought for glory; but he acquired it in a large degree compared to which that of Bonaparte is but a pale and uncertain glimmer to a noon-day blaze.[19]

Contemporaries who knew him expressed similar opinions. Talleyrand, for example (who had predeceased him by some fourteen years), stated that when all his public and personal matters were considered, he believed that Wellington was the greatest man that England, or any other country, ever produced. Such encomiums were only to be expected, especially in the immediate aftermath of his death, and tended to overlook the periods of unpopularity and the fact that during his period of military command officers under his command leveled a number of complaints against his plans and abilities.

Such criticisms should be considered in any objective assessment of the duke. In September 1810 Wellington commented acerbically on the circulation of complaints about him:

> [T]here is a system of croaking in the army which is highly injurious to the public service. . . . Officers have a right to form their own opinions upon events and transactions; but Officers of high rank or situation ought to keep their opinions to themselves: if they do not

approve of the system of operations of their commander, they ought
to withdraw from the army.[20]

(Ever confident of his own ability, he then added that only he had
kept the army in the Peninsula: "if any body else, knowing what I
do, had commanded the army, they [the complainers] would now
have been at Lisbon, if not in their ships"!) The level of "croaking"
probably represented a very small minority opinion; for example,
one experienced officer complained in 1811, "I am astonished to
see the ridiculous nonsense put in the English papers by the friends
of young men who are as ignorant as themselves,"[21] referring to letters from junior officers that had been publicized by their recipients.

Some of the criticisms may have arisen from ignorance of
Wellington's situation or of the wider context of the war, all but
invisible to junior officers serving at the regimental level ("the mag-
nitude of the concern is too much for their minds and their nerves,"
as Wellington had put it), or from perceived slights arising from
Wellington's habit of being parsimonious with his praise. It is worth
remarking that in August 1810 he wrote to Torrens, the commander
in chief's secretary, with a long complaint about his inability to
reward deserving officers with promotion. He acknowledged that
however desirable a system that restricted promotion to military
merit was, it was impossible to circumvent the influence of patronage; yet,

> I, who command the largest British army that has been employed
> against the enemy for many years, and who have upon my hands
> certainly the most expensive and difficult concern that was ever
> imposed upon any British officer, have not the power of making
> even a corporal!!!

He added that this complaint was not made because he wished to
exert patronage himself, for "I would not give one pin to have the
disposal of every commission in the army."[22]

On a purely personal level, his aloof exterior and brusque manner may have won few friends and were not calculated to engender

popularity. Orders that appeared harsh were often necessary, and at times the situation was sufficiently critical to cause Wellington to act in a manner that appeared tactless and unfair. For example, William Napier recalled an incident in 1812 when Wellington rode up "much displeased" with General Alten's dispositions and vented his spleen upon Napier instead:

> He was very angry, and reprimanded Alten who was near by by his mode of addressing me: 'What the devil are you about here with your squares?'; 'They are not my squares, they are General Alten's.' . . . 'Don't reply—order the division to retreat—and—do you hear, sir?— cover it with four companies of the 43rd and Riflemen.' I took the hint, and carried the order to Alten to retreat.[23]

In less stressful situations, however, he could be companionable toward subordinates, as a Guards officer discovered at dinner late in 1810:

> Although upon his acts depended the fate of nations, few, from observation, could discover that he felt himself in a more responsible position than the youngest subaltern of his army. He seemed to enjoy the boyish tricks of those about him; weighty affairs did not appear to have impaired his zest for the playfulness or jokes of his followers.[24]

William Napier's brother George must have recognized that upon a casual meeting, it may not always have been easy to warm to the duke as a man, but commented:

> Lord Wellington was placed in a very critical situation, and often found it necessary to be stern and inflexible in his administration of the army; and I am sure, though he is not a man who outwardly shows any softness of feeling, that he has always felt the greatest repugnance to ordering military executions or harsh treatment of either officers, soldiers, or inhabitants . . . the Duke of Wellington does not get the credit which is his due upon the score of feeling. He has a short manner of speaking and a stern look, which people

mistake for want of heart; but I have witnessed his kindness to others, and felt it myself in so many instances and so strongly, that I cannot bear to hear him accused of wanting what I know he possesses; as he has, by his own transcendent abilities, risen to the highest power and rank that a British subject can attain, so will there be found people always ready to detract from his merit, and try every means to sink him in public opinion.[25]

A similar comment on Wellington's manner was made in an assessment of the Duke published during his lifetime, in as much as

he had not, like Buonaparte [sic] and Nelson, the art of attaching men to him, or of exciting their enthusiasm. It must be admitted that his natural disposition was adverse to the use of cajoling speeches; that he was not so pliant and artful in this respect as Buonaparte.

The author excused this in part by Wellington's need to impose stricter discipline than did Napoleon, who

systematically supported his army by forced contributions and plunder; and as to drunkenness, which is the vice most hurtful to discipline, it is well known that the French soldiers (partly from national habit, and partly from their system of recruiting), are much less addicted to it than the English.[26]

Despite the number of "croakers" who complained about him, a far greater number shared the view of George Simmons of the Ninety-fifth, who wrote home in May 1811 to report that

Lord Wellington is adored by his army; wherever he is, confidence of success is the result. The French own that, next to Buonaparte [sic], he is the first Captain of Europe. I wish his lordship had Buonaparte to contend with instead of Massena; we should soon settle the business.[27]

Clearly the esteem he reported grew more from Wellington's military skills and the superintendence of his army, as only a relatively tiny minority would have had the opportunity to engage with him in person.

As a contrast to his military talents, in retrospect perceived flaws in Wellington's character might be debated at length. Lord Roberts of Kandahar, for example, himself a field marshal and a hero for a later generation of British soldiers, stated, "A study of Wellington's life and writings leads me to the conclusion that he has been somewhat overrated as a man and greatly underrated as a commander."[28] Rev. George Gleig, who knew the duke both as a commander (having served under him during the Peninsular War) and subsequently as a friend, so was not wholly unbiased, articulated a slightly different view. He wrote:

> The great leading principle of his moral being was—duty . . . as a public man, he had but one object in view, viz., to benefit, to the utmost of his ability and skill, the state, whose servant he was. . . . He was the grandest, because the truest man, whom modern times have produced. He was the wisest and most loyal subject that ever served and supported the English throne.[29]

Not entirely incompatible with this assessment was Lord Roberts's remark that he did not believe that, in the military sphere at least, Wellington's duty had ever conflicted with his own interests and personal advancement, so that the motivation was not wholly altruistic.

While the same sense of duty may have directed Wellington's political career, it had a markedly different outcome from the success of his military service and gave rise to his period of popular disapproval, including the alienation of some of those who should have shared his beliefs. It is, however, as a general that he is remembered, and the perspective of the ordinary soldiers who served under his command would not have been primarily of a dutiful public servant, even one described as "the greatest man of our age." Instead, they would have remembered a military commander of exceptional ability, a slim, remote figure in a plain frock coat and low cocked hat, with a hooked nose and a piercing eye that saw their own misdemeanors and discerned the enemy's tactics; a general who demonstrated genuine concern for their welfare, endeavored to keep them fed, and never risked their lives unnecessarily, and in whom they reposed immense faith in his ability to bring them victory. Writing of 1813, Harry Smith exemplified the morale generated by Wellington's superintendence of his army: "such was the ardour and confidence of our army at that moment, that, if Lord Wellington told us to carry the moon, we should have done it."[30]

Wellington himself was reported to have recalled an occasion in the Peninsular War, when he rode up to sort out a difficult situation; seeing him, one of the soldiers stepped from the ranks and called out, "Here comes the —— as knows how." It was entirely in character that the duke claimed that it was the greatest compliment he had ever received.[31]

Notes

Chapter 1

1. L. J. Jennings, ed., *The Croker Papers*, vol. 1 (London: John Murray, 1884), 12–13.

2. Questions surround both his date and place of birth: he always regarded May 1 as his birthday, though the principal cause of doubt is an entry in the register of St. Peter's Church, Dublin, claiming that he was baptized on April 30. The alternatives and sources are summarized in Philip Guedalla, *The Duke* (London: Hodder and Stoughton, 1937, first published 1931), 479–80.

3. J. F. Neville, *Leisure Moments in the Camp and Guard-Room* (York: Thomas Wilson & Son, 1812, published anonymously by "A Veteran British Officer"), 98.

4. *London Chronicle,* January 22, 1795.

5. Francis, First Earl Ellesmere, *Personal Reminiscences of the Duke of Wellington,* ed. Alice, Countess of Strafford (London: John Murray, 1904), 80.

6. Ibid., 161.

7. Philip Stanhope, Fifth Earl, *Notes of Conversations With the Duke of Wellington, 1831–1851* (London: John Murray, 1888), 182.

8. Ibid., 182.

9. Gen. Sir James Shaw Kennedy, *Notes on the Battle of Waterloo* (London: John Murray, 1865), 28.

10. George Elers, *The Memoirs of George Elers,* ed. Lord Monson and G. Leveson Gower (London: William Heinemann, 1903), 55–56.

Chapter 2

1. John Gurwood, ed., *The Dispatches of Field Marshal the Duke of Wellington During His Various Campaigns From 1799 to 1815*, vol. 1 (London: John Murray, 1834–38), 24.

2. Richard Bayly, *Diary of Colonel Bayly, 12th Regiment, 1796–1830* (London: Army Navy Co-Operative Society, 1896), 88–90.

3. Elers, *Memoirs*, 101.
4. W. H. Wilkin, *The Life of Sir David Baird* (London: George Allen, 1912), 89.
5. Seer: a measure of dry goods, usually about or slightly more than two pounds avoirdupois. Gurwood, *Dispatches*, 2:61.
6. Hircarrah: a guide. Gurwood, *Dispatches,* 2:62.
7. Gurwood, *Dispatches,* 2:210.
8. Ibid., 179.
9. Ibid., 404.
10. Ibid., 3:339.
11. Stanhope, *Notes*, 130.
12. Cutwahl: a chief officer of police and superintendent of bazaars. Gurwood, *Dispatches,* 2:372–3.
13. Ibid., 3:420.
14. Ibid., 2:563.
15. Elers, *Memoirs*, 121.
16. Second Duke of Wellington, ed., *Supplementary Despatches and Memoranda of Field-Marshal the Duke of Wellington*, vol. 4 (London: John Murray, 1858–72), 484.
17. Stanhope, *Notes*, 102.
18. Elers, *Memoirs*, 120–21.
19. Stanhope, *Notes*, 102.

Chapter 3
1. Gurwood, *Dispatches,* 4:2.
2. Elers, *Memoirs*, 126.
3. See Joan Wilson, *A Soldier's Wife: Wellington's Marriage* (London: Weidenfeld and Nicolson, 1987), 78.
4. *The Gentleman's Magazine,* August 1807, 764.
5. Stanhope, *Notes*, 69.
6. Ibid.
7. Gurwood, *Dispatches*, 4:30–31.
8. Ibid., 58–59.
9. Also styled "Rorica" in some sources and "Roleia" in battle honors until the spelling was changed to "Rolica" in 1911.
10. Sometimes styled "Vimiero" or "Vimiera."
11. Moyle Sherer, *Recollections of the Peninsula* (London: Longman, Hurst, Rees, Orme, Brown, and Green, 1825), 41–42; originally published as "by the Author of Sketches of India." This anecdote was reported second-hand.
12. Gurwood, *Dispatches*, 4:128.
13. Ibid., 136.
14. *The News,* November 6, 1808.

Chapter 4

1. Gurwood, *Dispatches,* 4:261.
2. G. C. Moore Smith, *The Life of John Colborne, Field-Marshal Lord Seaton, Compiled From His Letters, Records of His Conversations, and Other Sources* (London: John Murray, 1903), 130.
3. Sir William Warre, *Letters From the Peninsula, 1808–1812,* ed. Rev. Edmond Warre (London: John Murray, 1909), 74.
4. Gurwood, *Dispatches*, 4:515, 528.
5. Ibid., 526.
6. Ibid., 543.
7. Ibid., 549.
8. Ibid., 5:11, 13.
9. Ibid., 4:554.
10. Ibid., 5:158.
11. J. Jones, "Memoranda Relative to the Lines Thrown up to Cover Lisbon in 1810," in *Papers Connected With the Duties of the Corps of Royal Engineers,* vol. 3 (London: John Weale, 1839), 38.
12. Gurwood, *Dispatches*, 10:569.
13. Ibid., 11:184–85.
14. Stanhope, *Notes*, 11, 90–91.
15. Ibid., 10, 91.
16. Gurwood, *Dispatches*, 6:429.
17. Stanhope, *Notes*, 60.
18. Sir Henry Bunbury, *Memoirs and Literary Remains of Lieutenant-General Sir Henry Edward Bunbury, Bt.,* ed. Sir Charles Bunbury (London: Spottiswoode, 1868), 295.
19. Gurwood, *Dispatches*, 6:475.
20. Ibid., 7:432.
21. Ibid., 519.
22. Wellington, *Supplementary Despatches,* 7:117.
23. Ibid., 123.
24. Gurwood, *Dispatches*, 8:51.
25. Arthur Griffiths, *The Wellington Memorial* (London: George Allen, 1897), 307–8.
26. Gurwood, *Dispatches*, 7:558.
27. Ibid., 569.

Chapter 5

1. *Edinburgh Evening Courant*, December 1, 1810.
2. Ellesmere, *Personal Reminiscences*, 78.
3. George R. Gleig, *The Subaltern* (Edinburgh: William Blackwood and Sons, 1872), 66–67.
4. Gurwood, *Dispatches,* 7:371–72.

5. William Grattan, *Adventures With the Connaught Rangers* (London: Colburn, 1847; reprinted, ed. Sir Charles Oman, 1902), 50.

6. Gurwood, *Dispatches,* 10:209.

7. Stanhope, *Notes,* 29.

8. Ibid., 69.

9. Wellington, *Supplementary Despatches,* 10:219.

10. Gurwood, *Dispatches,* 7:35.

11. Ibid., 8:417.

12. Griffiths, *The Wellington Memorial,* 308.

13. Ibid., 295.

14. Sir William Fraser, *Words on Wellington* (London: J. C. Nimmo, 1889), 182.

15. Francis S. Larpent, *The Private Journal of Judge-Advocate Larpent* (London: Bentley, 1854), 85.

16. Sir James McGrigor, *The Autobiography and Services of Sir James McGrigor, Bart., Late Director-General of the Army Medical Department* (London: Longman, Green, Longman and Roberts, 1861), 302.

17. Gurwood, *Dispatches,* 10:77.

18. Ibid., 9:52.

19. *Edinburgh Evening Courant,* August 24, 1812.

20. Fraser, *Words on Wellington,* 37.

21. Thomas Creevey, *The Creevey Papers,* ed. Sir J. Maxwell (London: John Murray, 1904), 228.

22. Gurwood, *Dispatches,* 11:34–35.

23. *The Gentleman's Magazine,* July 1814, 79.

24. Stanhope, *Notes,* 18.

25. Col. W. K. Stuart, *Reminiscences of a Soldier*, vol. 2 (London: Hurst and Blackett, 1874), 276.

26. Frederick H. Pattison, *Personal Recollections of the Waterloo Campaign* (Glasgow: privately published, 1873), 26.

27. Stanhope, *Notes,* 18.

28. Anonymous, "Journal of an Officer, Belonging to the English Army in Spain," *The Monthly Magazine,* November 1, 1809, 353.

29. William Tomkinson, *The Diary of a Cavalry Officer in the Peninsular War and Waterloo Campaign, 1809–1815,* ed. J. Tomkinson (London: Swan Sonnenschein, 1895), 117.

30. Sir John Kincaid, *Random Shots From a Rifleman* (1835), reprinted in combined edition with *Adventures in the Rifle Brigade* (1830) (London: Maclaren, 1908), 245–46.

31. Gleig, *The Subaltern,* 67–68.

32. B. Smyth, *History of the XX Regiment, 1688–1888* (London: Simpkin, Marshall, 1889), 396.

33.   Kincaid, *Random Shots*, 36–37.

34.   John S. Cooper, *Rough Notes of Seven Campaigns in Portugal, Spain, France, and America* (Carlisle: G. and T. Coward, 1914), 68.

Chapter 6

1.   Sir William (W. F. P.) Napier, *History of the War in the Peninsula*, vol. 3 (London: Thomas and William Boone, 1832–40), 525–26.

2.   Fraser, *Words on Wellington*, 181.

3.   Kincaid, *Random Shots*, 66.

4.   Gurwood, *Dispatches,* 9:227.

5.   Ibid., 43.

6.   Ibid., 270.

7.   Ibid., 309–10.

8.   Napier, *History,* 5:167.

9.   Sir Herbert Maxwell, *The Life of Wellington: The Restoration of the Martial Power of Great Britain*, vol. 1 (London: Sampson Low, Marston, 1899), 282.

10.   Ellesmere, *Personal Reminiscences*, 108.

11.   Gurwood, *Dispatches,* 9:395.

12.   *Edinburgh Evening Courant,* August 24, 1812.

13.   Gurwood, *Dispatches,* 9:310.

14.   Ibid., 373–74.

15.   Ibid., 566.

16.   Ellesmere, *Personal Reminiscences*, 146.

17.   Gurwood, *Dispatches,* 9:394.

18.   Ibid., 519.

19.   See I. Fletcher, ed., *For King and Country: The Letters and Diaries of John Mills, Coldstream Guards, 1811–14* (Staplehurst: Spellmount, 1995), 253; and C. T. Atkinson, ed., "A Peninsular Brigadier: Letters of Major-General Sir F. P. Robinson KCB, Dealing With the Campaign of 1813," *Journal of the Society for Army Historical Research* 34 (December 1956): 158–59.

20.   Gurwood, *Dispatches,* 9:565.

21.   Ibid., 10:492.

22.   Ibid., 602.

23.   Ibid., 11:124.

24.   Ibid., 69.

25.   Ibid., 306–7.

26.   Ibid., 391.

27.   Sir Harry Smith, *The Autobiography of Sir Harry Smith, 1787–1819,* ed. G. C. Moore Smith (London: John Murray, 1910), 143.

28.   Moore Smith, *The Life of John Colborne,* 198–9.

29. Gurwood, *Dispatches,* 11:568–69.
30. Sir William Napier, *Life of General Sir William Napier, KCB*, vol. 1, ed. H. A. Bruce (London: John Murray, 1864), 165–66.
31. Stanhope, *Notes*, 31.
32. Larpent, *Private Journal*, 227.
33. Gurwood, *Dispatches,* 11:668.
34. Emmanuel A. D. M. J. Las Cases, *Memoirs of the Life, Exile and Conversations of the Emperor Napoleon*, vol. 2 (London: Henry Colburn, 1834), 134–35, 296.

Chapter 7

1. *The Gentleman's Magazine,* May 1811, 487.
2. Gurwood, *Dispatches,* 12:62.
3. Ibid., 65–66.
4. Ibid., 11:668.
5. William Hay, *Reminiscences Under Wellington, 1808–1815*, ed. Mrs. S. C. I. Wood (London: Simpkin, Marshall, Hamilton, Kent, 1901), 158.
6. William Wheeler, *The Letters of Private Wheeler, 1809–1828,* ed. Capt. Basil H. Liddell Hart (London: Michael Joseph, 1951), 161.
7. Gurwood, *Dispatches,* 12:358.
8. Kincaid, *Random Shots*, 171.
9. Fraser, *Words on Wellington*, 186.
10. Ibid., 100.
11. Ibid., 367–68.
12. Gurwood, *Dispatches,* 12:375–76.
13. Ibid., 462.
14. Fraser, *Words on Wellington*, 3.
15. Sherer, *Recollections*, 151.
16. Sir Augustus Frazer, *Letters of Colonel Sir Augustus Simon Frazer KCB,* ed. Maj. Gen. E. Sabine (London: Longmans, 1859), 550, 559–60.
17. Kennedy, *Notes*, 128.
18. David Robertson, *Journal of Sergeant D. Robertson, Late 92nd Foot* (Perth: J. Fisher, 1842), 159.
19. Kincaid, *Random Shots*, 171.
20. Smith, *Autobiography*, 291.
21. Gurwood, *Dispatches,* 12:483.
22. Ibid., 529.

Chapter 8

1. Frazer, *Letters*, 529.

2. Lady Magdalene DeLancey, *A Week at Waterloo in 1815*, ed. Maj. B. R. Ward (London: John Murray, 1906), 77.

3. Fraser, *Words on Wellington*, 97.

4. Stanhope, *Notes*, 194.

5. Ibid., 120.

6. Maxwell, *The Life of Wellington*, 2:194.

7. Stanhope, *Notes*, 45.

8. Maxwell, *The Life of Wellington*, 2:234.

9. Fraser, *Words on Wellington*, 12.

10. Stanhope, *Notes*, 194.

11. Rev. G. R. Gleig, *The Life of Arthur Duke of Wellington* (London: Longmans, Green, Reader, and Dyer, 1865), 399.

12. Ibid., 398.

13. Maxwell, *The Life of Wellington*, 2:351.

14. Fraser, *Words on Wellington*, 108.

15. Ellesmere, *Personal Reminiscences*, 140.

16. Ibid., 236.

17. Quoted in Maxwell, *The Life of Wellington*, 2:93.

18. Fraser, *Words on Wellington*, 109.

19. *Illustrated London News,* no. 591 (November 20, 1852): 425–26.

20. Gurwood, *Dispatches,* 6:429.

21. George Simmons, *A British Rifle Man,* ed. Lt. Col. W. Verner (London: A. and C. Black, 1899), 181.

22. Gurwood, *Dispatches,* 6:326–27.

23. Napier, *Life,* 110–11.

24. John S. Cowell (later Cowell-Stepney), *Leaves From the Diary of an Officer of the Guards* (published anonymously) (London: Chapman and Hall, 1854), 36.

25. Sir George Napier, *Passages in the Early Military Life of General Sir George T. Napier, KCB, Written by Himself,* ed. Gen. W. C. E. Napier (London: John Murray, 1884), 168.

26. Anonymous, "The Duke of Wellington," *The United Service Journal and Naval and Military Magazine*, May 1840, 151.

27. Simmons, *British Rifle Man*, 183.

28. Frederick, Lord Roberts, *The Rise of Wellington* (London: Sampson Low, Marston, 1895), 185.

29. Gleig, *Life,* 461, 496.

30. Smith, *Autobiography*, 126.

31. F. E. Du Cane, "The Peninsula and Waterloo: Memories of an Old Rifleman," *Cornhill Magazine*, December 1897, 751.

Bibliography

The following lists works relating primarily to the Duke of Wellington himself and his army, not including the many works that cover his campaigns in general.

Anonymous. *Wellington Anecdotes: A Collection of Sayings and Doings of the Great Duke*. London: Petter, Duff, 1852.

Brett-James, Antony, ed. *Wellington at War: A Selection of His Wartime Letters*. London: Macmillan, 1961.

Bryant, Sir Arthur. *The Great Duke*. London: Collins, 1971.

Burghclere, Lady, ed. *A Great Man's Friendship: Letters of the Duke of Wellington to Mary, Marchioness of Salisbury, 1850–1852*. London: John Murray, 1927.

Chad, George W. *The Conversations of the First Duke of Wellington with George William Chad*. Edited by Seventh Duke of Wellington. Cambridge: Saint Nicholas Press, 1956.

Cooper, Leonard. *The Age of Wellington: The Life and Times of the Duke of Wellington*. London: Macmillan, 1964.

Eimer, Christopher. *Medallic Portraits of the Duke of Wellington*. London: Spink, 1994.

Ellesmere, Francis, First Earl, *Personal Reminiscences of the Duke of Wellington*. Edited by Alice, Countess of Stafford. London: John Murray, 1904.

Fraser, Sir William, Bt. *Words on Wellington: The Duke; Waterloo; the Ball*. London: John C. Nimmo, 1889.

Gleig, Rev. George R. *The Life of Arthur Duke of Wellington*. London: Longmans, Green, Reader, and Dyer, 1865.

Glover, Michael. *Wellington as Military Commander*. London: Batsford, 1968.

———. *Wellington's Army in the Peninsula, 1808–1814*. Newton Abbot: David and Charles, 1977.

Griffith, Paddy, ed. *Wellington Commander: The Iron Duke's Generalship*. Chichester: Anthony Bird, 1985.

Griffiths, Maj. Arthur. *Wellington and Waterloo*. London: George Newnes, 1898.

———. *The Wellington Memorial*. London: George Allen, 1897.

Guedalla, Philip. *The Duke*. London: Hodder and Stoughton, 1931.

Haythornthwaite, Philip J. *The Armies of Wellington*. London: Arms and Armour Press, 1994.

Hibbert, Christopher. *Wellington: A Personal History*. London: Harper Collins, 1997.

Holmes, Richard. *Wellington: The Iron Duke*. London: Harper Collins, 2002.

James, Lawrence. *The Iron Duke: A Military Biography of Wellington*. London: Weidenfeld and Nicolson, 1992.

Lennox, Lord William. *Three Years With the Duke, or Wellington in Private Life*. London: Sanders and Otley, 1853.

Longford, Elizabeth, Countess of. *Wellington: Pillar of State*. London: Weidenfeld and Nicolson, 1972.

———. *Wellington: The Years of the Sword*. London: Weidenfeld and Nicolson, 1969.

Maxwell, Sir Herbert, Bt. *The Life of Wellington: The Restoration of the Martial Power of Great Britain*. London: Sampson Low, Marston, 1899.

Maxwell, W. H. *Life of Field-Marshal His Grace the Duke of Wellington*. London: H. H. Bailey, 1839–41.

Oman, Sir Charles. *Wellington's Army, 1809–1814*. London: Edward Arnold, 1913.

Petrie, Sir Charles, Bt. *Wellington: A Reassessment*. London: James Barrie, 1956.

Physick, John. *The Duke of Wellington in Caricature*. London: HMSO, 1965.

Roberts, Andrew. *Napoleon and Wellington*. London: Weidenfeld and Nicolson, 2001.

Roberts, Gen. Frederick, First Earl. *The Rise of Wellington*. London: Sampson Low, Marston, 1895.

Rogers, Col. H. C. B. *Wellington's Army*. London: Ian Allan, 1979.

Stanhope, Philip Henry, Fifth Earl. *Notes of Conversations With the Duke of Wellington, 1831–1851*. London: John Murray, 1888.

Ward, S. G. P. *Wellington*. London: Batsford, 1963.

———. *Wellington's Headquarters: A Study of the Administrative Problems in the Peninsula, 1809–1814*. Oxford: Oxford University Press, 1957.

Weller, Jac. *On Wellington: The Duke and His Art of War*. Edited by Andrew Uffindell. London: Greenhill, 1998.

———. *Wellington at Waterloo*. London: Longmans, 1967.

———. *Wellington in India*. London: Longmans, 1972.

———. *Wellington in the Peninsula*. London: Nicholas Vane, 1962.

Wellington, Arthur, First Duke. *The Despatches of Field-Marshal the Duke of Wellington*. Edited by Walter Wood (London: Grant Richards, 1902).

———. *The Dispatches of Field Marshal the Duke of Wellington During His Various Campaigns*. Edited by Lt.-Col. J. Gurwood. London: John Murray, 1834–38.

———. *The General Orders of Field Marshal the Duke of Wellington, in Portugal, Spain, and France, From 1809 to 1814; in the Low Countries and France in 1815; and in France, Army of Occupation, From 1816 to 1818*. Edited by Lt.-Col. J. Gurwood. London: H. Clowes and Son, 1837.

———. *Supplementary Despatches and Memoranda of Field Marshal Arthur Duke of Wellington, K.G.* Edited by Second Duke of Wellington. London: John Murray, 1858–72.

———. *Wellington and His Friends: Letters of the First Duke of Wellington to the Rt. Hon. Charles and Mrs. Arbuthnot, the Earl and Countess of Wilton, Princess Lieven, and Miss Burdett-Coutts*. Edited by Seventh Duke of Wellington. London: Macmillan, 1965.

Woolgar, C. M., ed. *Wellington Studies*. Southampton: University of Southampton, 1996.

About the Author

Philip Haythornthwaite was born in Lancashire, England, the county in which he still lives. Fascinated by all aspects of history from an early age, he began to write about military history soon after completing his education while pursuing a career in business. He is the author of many books, articles, and papers and has a wide knowledge of military subjects of the eighteenth and nineteenth centuries, notably the era of the Napoleonic Wars, which has always held a special attraction. At least one ancestor served under Wellington's command in the Peninsula and at Waterloo.

Among his publications especially relevant to this study of Wellington are *The Armies of Wellington, The Napoleonic Source Book, Wellington's Military Machine, Waterloo Men: The Experience of Battle, Brassey's Almanac of the Peninsular War, Wellington's Army: The Uniforms of the British Soldier, 1812–1815,* and two volumes on the weapons and tactics of the period, *Napoleonic Cavalry* and *Napoleonic Infantry.* Other notable works include *The World War One Source Book* and *The Colonial Wars Source Book.* He has edited and provided introductions for the reissue of a number of memoirs from the Napoleonic era, including some of those who fought both for and against Wellington.